Early Praise for *Believe for It*

"CeCe is a powerful woman of God who lives her faith on-stage and off. Her personal story and message of her faith in God is inspiring and something we need more than ever in our world today. I believe her book will help both older and younger generations who want to be authentic followers of Jesus and draw others to Christ!"

—Joyce Meyer, Bible teacher and bestselling author

"CeCe Winans and her family are treasured friends in ministry with me, my children, and she was especially a great friend over the years with my deceased wife, Lois Evans. The Kingdom work I have witnessed them leading and being a part of has spanned decades in multiple generations. That is the heart and biblical wisdom of what CeCe shares in *Believe for It*. My prayer is that this book helps people see what God can do through intentionality in family, church community, and fervent prayer."

—Dr. Tony Evans, President, The Urban Alternative, Senior Pastor, Oak Cliff Bible Fellowship

"My friend CeCe Winans is a gifted and beloved Gospel recording artist, and she has written a new book that is refreshing and needed today. In a culture that is heavy-laden with failed marriages and broken homes, CeCe writes about the hope that Jesus Christ brings into family life when parents and children honor the Lord through obedience to His Word. Her own story will inspire and capture anew what happens when Christ is put at the center of our hearts and homes. No matter what has happened in life, it is never too late to '*Believe for It*.'"

—Franklin Graham, President and CEO, Billy Graham Evangelistic Association, Samaritan's Purse

"I believe in the power of what God can do through family. What my friend CeCe Winans has done in '*Believe for It*' shows how God uses generations to pass down faith."

—Bishop T. D. Jakes, *New York Times* bestselling author

BELIEVE
for it

Passing On Faith *to the* Next Generation

CECE WINANS
with Suzanne Gosselin

K-LOVE
BOOKS

FRANKLIN, TENNESSEE

K-LOVE. BOOKS

K-LOVE Books
West Oaks Blvd.
Rocklin, CA 95765

Unless otherwise noted, scripture quotations are taken from The Holy Bible, New International Version®, NIV® Copyright ©1973, 1978, 1984, 2011 by Biblica, Inc.® Used by permission. All rights reserved worldwide.

Scripture quotations marked ESV are taken from The Holy Bible, English Standard Version. ESV® Text Edition: 2016. Copyright © 2001 by Crossway Bibles, a publishing ministry of Good News Publishers.

Scripture quotations marked NCV are taken from The Holy Bible, New Century Version®. Copyright © 2005 by Thomas Nelson, Inc.

Scripture quotations marked NKJV are taken from the New King James Version®. Copyright © 1982 by Thomas Nelson. Used by permission. All rights reserved.

"He is Concerned" Courtesy of Kayla Music Publishing, written by Kayla Denise Parker

Printed in the United States of America.

First edition: 2022
10 9 8 7 6 5 4 3 2 1

ISBN: 978-1-954201-34-7 (Hardcover)
ISBN: 978-1-954201-37-8 (Trade Paperback)
ISBN: 978-1-954201-35-4 (E-book)
ISBN: 978-1-954201-36-1 (Audiobook)

Publisher's Cataloging-in-Publication Data

Names: Winans, CeCe, author. | Gosselin, Suzanne, author.
Title: Believe for it : passing on faith to the next generation / CeCe Winans; with Suzanne Gosselin.
Description: Rocklin, CA: K-LOVE Books, 2022.
Identifiers: ISBN: 978-1-954201-34-7 (hardcover) | 978-1-954201-35-4 (ebook) | 978-1-954201-36-1 (audio)
Subjects: LCSH Winans, CeCe. | Christian life. | Self-actualization (Psychology)--Religious aspects--Christianity. | BISAC RELIGION / Christian Living / Inspirational | RELIGION / Inspirational | SELF-HELP / Spiritual
Classification: LCC BV4598.2 .W565 2022| DDC 248.4--dc23

Cover design by Charissa Newell
Cover photo by CMON Creative
Interior design by PerfecType, Nashville, TN

DEDICATION

I dedicate this book to my mom, Delores Winans.
Thank you for being a perfect pattern to model my life after.
Your beauty and grace intensifies with each passing day.

CONTENTS

INTRODUCTION

I was the eighth child born in my family, but I was the first Winans.

Though my heritage is rich and faith filled, my family tree isn't picture perfect. My father, David, was conceived out of wedlock and raised by a single mother, Laura Glenn. Since his father, Carvin Winans, wasn't in the picture when he was growing up, my father went by the surname Glenn. So when my seven older brothers—David, Ronald, Marvin, Carvin, Michael, Daniel, and Benjamin (BeBe) came along—they were born Glenns.

My great-grandfather Isaiah Winans came from Mississippi. He was a bishop in the Church of God in Christ and founded Zion Congregational Church of God in Christ in Detroit, Michigan. A short time before I was born, my great-grandfather approached my dad and requested that he take the name Winans. Even though my dad's father hadn't been present during much of his life, my dad consented to his grandfather's wishes out of respect. And that's how I earned the bragging rights of being the first child of my family to be born a Winans.

I have always appreciated my rich Christian heritage. I think that's why I'm passionate about influencing the next generation. We have all been influenced by those who came before us. Along with faith, music played a big role in my upbringing. I suppose it's fitting that music is what brought my dad and mom together. They met in 1950 as members of the Lemon Gospel Chorus, a citywide gospel choir led by gospel great Louise Lemon.

Dad and Mom married in 1953 at the tender ages of nineteen and seventeen. Music was a part of their home, even before my oldest brother was born the following year. Mom played the piano, Dad played the saxophone, and both had impressive singing voices. (Later in their lives they would record several albums together.) Before children came along, both had traveled half the country in a handful of musical groups, so I suppose it's no surprise their children followed in their footsteps.

A large family wasn't part of my parents' plan. Mom used to tell us, "I only planned to have two children, a boy and a girl. It's just that the girl was slow in coming." Clearly God had different ideas. In 1964, I was born Priscilla Marie Winans. Priscilla was the beautiful baby girl name my mom had been saving up in her heart through all those years of having sons. Sometime early in my childhood, "CeCe" became my nickname. By 1972,

God had blessed my parents with two more daughters, Angelique (Angie) and Deborah (Debbie), completing the Winans family.

I remember two major things about my childhood. The first is that our home was always filled with music. Gospel music played throughout our house morning and night. Most of my siblings played the piano and wrote songs—or at least they thought they could—so someone was always either playing the piano, writing a song, or rehearsing for a program. It seems we were singing before we learned to talk.

The second thing I remember is the faith that surrounded me; it was as strong and consistent as the air I breathed. My parents' commitment to the Lord and His Word enveloped us and guided everything we did. He was unequivocally the center of our home.

Dad came from a broken home and so did Mom. Her mother and her father weren't believers, nor were they married. Mom says she used to dread weekends when drunkenness and fighting broke out. Despite their fractured beginnings, my parents vowed together that they would stay married and raise their children to fear the Lord.

I was blessed to have a front-row seat to the power of this faith and commitment. By the way my dad and mom raised us, you would think the whole family tree was filled with saints. But no, like all families, we had our issues and generational curses. Our family may have been close knit (and still is), but that doesn't mean we didn't find ways to mess things up! For me, the beauty of the Winans story is that one act—my parents committing themselves, their marriage, and their family to God. It changed everything.

Through the years, as I've raised my own family— and seen my siblings raise theirs—I've realized to an even greater degree that no family is perfect. Not only that, but the world has become a difficult place in which to pass on authentic faith and a solid identity in Christ. Still, I am totally convinced God honors our commitment to Him and prayers for the next generation. My parents are an example of that. They raised ten children who not only loved to sing, but who grew up to sing God's praises.

Such a foundation is of immeasurable worth. The seeds of faith and service and discipline my parents planted in me have continued to grow and bear fruit throughout my life. God makes no secret of His plan for faith to be passed from generation to generation. Psalm 78:4 proclaims, "We will tell the next generation the praiseworthy deeds of the LORD, his power, and the wonders he has done."

No matter the condition of your family of origin or your current situation, passing on faith to the next gener- ation is possible. Establishing a loving, faithful household centered on Christ is not out of reach! After all, God used two teenagers committing their marriage and home to Him to raise up a family that would proclaim His wonders and glorious deeds around the world in ways that this young couple never could have imagined.

Even if you don't have children of your own, or your children are grown and out of the home, God calls you to participate in this calling as well. In Old Testament times, the charge was delivered to the community, to the people of God.

I hope to encourage you through my story and the things God has taught me along the way, from growing up a Winans to becoming an acclaimed gospel singer to getting married to raising two beautiful children of my own to founding a church. Our God is big and has a heart for all generations to believe in Him and be part of His big story. I pray this book helps you discover new ways of passing on powerful faith to the next generation.

The time is now! The apostle Peter said, "The end of all things is near. Therefore, be alert and of sober mind so that you may pray" (1 Peter 4:7). Our world has never been more in need of truth and the power of God's Holy Spirit. Old, young, or in between, every one of us has a limited time on this earth to establish a legacy of faith in the next generation. Let's roll up our sleeves and get to work.

CHAPTER

• *one* •

GENERATIONS

Ten years ago, in 2012, my husband, Alvin, and I started a church. It's still a bit shocking for me to write those words. Looking in from the outside, it seems extremely unlikely that we, a couple with no seminary training quickly approaching retirement, one day decided to convert our living room into what would become Nashville Life Church.

Looking back, God had been hounding us for fifteen years. At that time, we attended a revival at Born Again Church, our home church of more than twenty years. That night, a woman of God whom we respect prayed over Alvin and proclaimed he would be a pastor.

I remember shouting, "Oh, no!" I'm not sure why that was my gut-level response. I don't carry any deep hurt from growing up in the church—in fact, quite the opposite. But I knew the weight and responsibility of such a calling. I also didn't believe a businessman and a gospel singer were equipped for such a task.

Alvin, ever calm and levelheaded, had a different reaction. "She missed it," he said simply. "I would walk on the moon before I'd be pastor." And that was that. Only it wasn't. Over the next decade and a half, as I enjoyed a successful music career and we raised our children, God continued to keep the woman's words on our minds.

A stranger would approach us at the shopping mall. "You're a pastor," he would say to Alvin.

"No, I'm not," my husband would reply.

Stranger: "Oh, yes you are!"

Alvin: "Well, whatever the Lord wants. Praise the Lord!"

These chance encounters steadily grew through the years until it became almost ridiculous how many people mistook my husband for a pastor. We began to wonder what God had in store and even wondered if we would pastor those in the music industry. About a year before we founded Nashville Life, the prophecies were coming so frequently we could not ignore them.

We decided to pray about it: "If it's your will, Lord, we'll do whatever you want us to do. But this is a serious calling."

The catalyst came through our son, Alvin III. He was in his midtwenties at the time and going through a crisis of faith. He moved to Melbourne, Australia, to get some distance from us and to do his own thing. At that time, Alvin was consumed with his music. He had earned a music degree from Belmont University and was passionate about writing and producing. He entered competitions and wrote music that was secular. As I watched him spend time with friends who weren't living for Jesus, I knew something was off with his walk. He was searching for what he believed apart from Alvin and myself.

When Alvin III announced he was going to Australia, we were concerned about him being so far away. I prayed that God would bring him home, but I had no idea all that was at stake.

My son later told me, "Mom, I told God, 'Whoever gets me first, You or the devil, that's the way I'm going to go." Praise the Lord, God got him first!

When his friend, Wally, picked him up at the airport, he told Alvin about the discipleship ministry school he was attending at Melbourne Life Christian Church. Because he had no other plans, Alvin reluctantly agreed to join him. At the ministry school, God lit fire to Alvin's faith. Every time he called home, he seemed to have a more exciting story than the call before about what God was doing in his life.

My prayers of, "Lord, bring my son home," changed instantly to, "Lord, you can keep him there for as long as you want. In fact, it's fine if he never comes back as long as you're working in his life."

After about nine months, Alvin returned to Nashville. He was on fire for the Lord and wanted his friends in Tennessee to experience what he had in Melbourne. He asked if we could invite Dianne and Bram Manusama, the pastors of Melbourne Life Christian Church and the leaders of the Discipleship Ministry School, to our home in Nashville to lead a weeklong Bible study for a few of his friends. Alvin and I agreed immediately. When we asked the Manusamas to come, they weren't surprised. God had already revealed to them that He was planning to use them to further His kingdom in Nashville.

Our son asked us if he could invite twenty of his friends, which we said was just fine. But on the first day of the event, forty-five showed up, packing into our living room and kitchen! These young people were hungry for God's Word and His touch in their lives. That week God did a mighty work. As Dianne and Bram taught and the young people read the Word together, many were overcome by the Spirit and wept in repentance. They received healing and deliverance from addiction, anger, unforgiveness, and fear. At the end of the week, my husband told the young people to hold on to what God had given them.

"Go back to your church," he said. "And if you don't have a church, find one."

Both my husband and I knew the importance of being plugged into a faith community. Many of the young adults who had come to our home did not attend church. We knew without believers surrounding them that what they had experienced that week could easily fade away. Like the parable of the sower and the seeds, these precious souls would face many challenges to their faith as they forged a new path. That's why my husband encouraged them to continue their journeys sheltered by the fellowship of a local church.

Three months after that event, Alvin III asked if we could do it again. Those who had been transformed during the first event had spread the word, and more people wanted to come. The Manusamas returned to minister, and God did it again! More young people experienced transformation through the Word, the Holy Spirit, prayer, and repentance. As my husband observed what God was doing, Pastor Dianne looked at him and said, "This is your church."

My husband, Alvin, revealed to me later that he had made a specific request to the Lord: *If starting a church is Your will, bring it to our living room.* And that's exactly what the Lord did.

At the end of the event, Alvin said to the group, "Those of you who are part of a church, go back and stay on fire for God. If you don't have a church home, raise your hand." About thirty hands went up. And that is how Nashville Life Church began, meeting first in our living room and later at Wallace Chapel on the property of Christ Church Nashville.

During the years we met there, the pastors of Christ Church offered us such beautiful hospitality, an expression of the unity of the body of Christ. They made everything easy for us. I think God knew we needed everything to be easy in the beginning so we wouldn't give up.

A NEW PURPOSE

In those early days of Nashville Life, God revealed something significant to Alvin and me. The ethnically diverse group of millennials who streamed to our church had a deep need for God's transforming power in their lives. Many came from broken homes, and some of their families were not comprised of Spirit-filled believers. They needed spiritual parents and were drawn to Alvin and me.

We came to find out that only six out of ten in the millennial generation were raised by both parents.[1] Roughly 40 percent were missing a dad or mom in the home while growing up.

Research shows that in weighing their own priorities, the next generation places parenthood and marriage far above financial or career success. The young people filling our pews longed to see a model of a strong, loving marriage. They craved the security and acceptance we could offer. They desired parental figures who could guide them spiritually, hold them accountable, and support them. And they found those things in Alvin and me. In those earlier days, pastoring looked more like parenting, but it bore much fruit.

I thought back to my mom and dad. Though part of the silent generation, with the Lord's help, they had reversed the curse of a fractured family and given my nine siblings and me the blessings of a loving home centered

---

1. Russell Heimlich, "Missing Mom or Dad," Pew Research Center, March 22, 2010, www.pewresearch.org/fact-tank /2010/03/22/missing-mom-or-dad/.

on Christ. This idea of older generations passing down faith to the younger is not a new idea. Scripture contains more than 150 references to generations. Consider a few:

Let this be written for a future generation, that a
people not yet created may praise the LORD.
(Psalm 102:18)

One generation shall praise Your works to
another and shall declare Your mighty acts.
(Psalm 145:4, NKJV)

His mercy extends to those who fear him, from
generation to generation. (Luke 1:50)

Even when I am old and gray, do not forsake me,
my God, till I declare your power to the next generation, your mighty acts to all who are to come.
(Psalm 71:18)

I particularly love that last one. The psalmist expressly asks the Lord to be with him in his old age so that he may declare God's power to the next generation. As I walked alongside the young people in our church, this was my prayer too—that God would allow me to pass on faith to those who are to come.

The charge to parents to pass on faith to their children appears early in Scripture. We see a perfect example of this teaching in Deuteronomy 6. Just after presenting the Ten Commandments, Moses orders the people—every generation—to honor the Lord and obey His commands. He says, "Always remember these commands I give you today. Teach them to your children, and talk about them when you sit at home and walk along the road, when you lie down and when you get up" (6:6–7, NCV).

Passing on faith to the next generation is to be an immersive, all-of-life activity. Parents are to talk to their children about God constantly. They are to aggressively teach them the truth every day, every opportunity they get, so that their children will know the truth from the counterfeit.

When I think about my own upbringing, this method happened naturally in our home. The Winans kids were in church at least three days a week (more if there was a shut-in or revival). When we weren't at school or church, we were in the home singing gospel music, hearing the Word as part of family discussions, or preparing to serve in some way. We had fun and the usual family antics, of

Passing on faith
to the next generation
is to be an immersive,
all-of-life activity.

course, but faith was a natural and prevalent part of our lives. Even at a young age, when I had a problem, I knew to pray and seek the Lord's wisdom. When my siblings and I engaged in the usual arguments (and we did), we understood that God wanted us to forgive each other so that we could be forgiven. And when Mom or Dad put forth an edict, their word was law, and we honored it.

Passing on faith looked a little different when I was raising my own children, but Alvin and I made church a priority, and we made sure to make God's Word and His ways central to our household. Looking back, we could have done more, but I'm thankful for God's grace in allowing us to raise a son and daughter who know the Lord and follow Him despite our shortcomings.

When my children were grown, I was tempted to believe that my job was complete. I hoped to one day be a grandmother pouring into my grandbabies, as my own Grandmother Howze had done for me, but it felt like I had checked the Deuteronomy 6 box. What God began to show me was that the command to tell the next generation about who God is and about His plan for humanity extends beyond the nuclear family. Don't get me wrong—the nuclear family is a powerful vessel for transmitting authentic faith. However, Scripture is clear that this task is to be a community effort.

In Jewish culture each celebration and feast includes teachings for the children about who God is and what He has done. During the Feast of Passover, the children ask questions, which are answered by their elders. In the New Testament, we see that part of the function of the church is to provide a community where older generations teach the younger ones. Passing on the faith is not something that happens by osmosis. Quite the contrary. The task requires consistent, diligent, prayerful effort from both the parents and the entire faith community.

GENERATIONS

Pastoring a diverse church of millennials was a wake-up call. I began to realize that the greatest thing I could leave to my children is my faith. The best investment of my time would be in pursuits that would result in the next generation being grounded in faith. As I witnessed the great need for spiritual investment in those who attended our church, I felt a sense of urgency to be a part of this important work of passing on faith.

In 2021, God put it on my heart to create a YouTube show called *Generations* to serve as a platform to invest in the spiritual lives of the next generation. Watching my son and his friends experience God in our living room and kitchen inspired me to create a casual, homey environment for the show. Each episode features me and my guests—often my mother, my daughter, and my sisters—gathered around in the kitchen, coffee cups in hand.

We discuss topics such as walking in faith, pursuing wholeness, honoring those who deserve honor, practicing gratitude, and celebrating holidays. The purpose of these discussions about life and faith is to start conversations that reflect the words of Titus 2:3–5:

> In the same way, teach older women to be holy in their behavior, not speaking against others or enslaved to too much wine, but teaching what is good. Then they can teach the young women to love their husbands, to love their children, to be wise and pure, to be good workers at home, to be kind, and to yield to their husbands. Then no one will be able to criticize the teaching God gave us. (NCV)

Whew! That's powerful. We teach those who are younger how to walk out their faith so that no one will be able to criticize the teaching God gave us. What a holy calling. But the exchange of wisdom goes both ways. Scripture reminds us that we who are seasoned saints can also learn from those who are young. In God's kingdom the aged don't have a corner on the market when it comes to spiritual knowledge and insight. The apostle Paul exhorted the young pastor Timothy, saying, "Do not let anyone treat you as if you are unimportant because you are young. Instead, be an example to the believers with your words, your actions, your love, your faith, and your pure life" (1 Timothy 4:12, NCV).

That's why I've invited my daughter, Ashley, and other young guests onto the show to share the wisdom God has given them as my brothers and sisters in Christ. We can all learn from each other. I regularly receive insight and a fresh perspective from these younger believers.

The *Generations* show grew into the Generations conference, which brought together women of faith of all ages to teach God's Word and pass on knowledge that will help the next generation thrive in faith. Through the show and the conference, we initiate conversations about how faith plays an important part in every area of life.

Psalm 119:105 tells us that God's Word is a lamp for our feet and a light on our path. The truth of that statement isn't limited to one culture or one demographic—it's for everybody of every age all over the world. God's wisdom and His way of doing things offers us the best paths to walk our life. It's vital for the younger generations to grasp that, and it's vital that the older generations convey their knowledge and experience on the matter.

Today I'm part of the older generation, but it seems like just yesterday I was part of the younger one. I was a young woman, beginning my music career, learning how to be a wife and mother, receiving from the older women in my life. How grateful I am for their investment in me as I learned to walk with the Spirit and grow deeper in faith. Their influence fortified me on the path God had for me.

But time passes quickly. As a young person you may be primarily on the receiving end, and if you're not careful, you'll stay in that position and forget the responsibility God has given you to pour into the next generation. I think some of us in our fifties, sixties, and beyond have become stuck. Instead of looking for ways to actively declare God's power to the next generation, we worry about feeling respected and comfortable at church.

Before Alvin and I founded Nashville Life Church, we were considering retirement and taking a long trip to Hawaii. Those plans quickly changed as we pressed into the adventure God was calling us to. My good friend Dr. Bridget Hilliard has said, "In God's kingdom there's not retiring, only restructuring." This has been very true of mine and Alvin's last decade. As I've come to better understand God's call on every believer to pass on faith, I have realized that stepping into this role of nurturing the faith of the next generation is a lifelong pursuit.

THE TIME IS NOW

Several years ago, I felt a growing sense of urgency. After nearly forty years of singing and touring, I felt a pull toward teaching and making disciples like I never had before. I continued to make music, but God was doing a new thing in me. Through my service at Nashville Life, I saw the incredible fruit that came from investing in young people and the benefits we all gained from intergenerational relationships.

Psalm 90:12 says, "Teach us how short our lives really are so that we may be wise" (NCV). That is exactly what God has impressed on my heart. By His blessing I have enjoyed a fruitful career in gospel and contemporary Christian music that has given me opportunities beyond what I could have imagined. But now is not the time to rest on my laurels. Just the opposite.

One of the reasons I am so passionate about the message of the importance of generations is because I sense the battle we're in. Ephesians 6:12 says, "For our struggle is not against flesh and blood, but against the rulers, against the authorities, against the powers of this dark world and against the spiritual forces of evil in the heavenly realms." I find it interesting that the phrase "flesh and blood" is used in this passage. It denotes that our battle is not physical, but in our culture it also carries the meaning of our blood relations. God is calling us not to engage in battle with the next generation, but to fight *for it*, against the forces of evil.

You don't have to look far to see the victories the enemy is winning in the lives of our youth. From bullying and mental health issues to addiction and suicide, the next generation faces some significant challenges. Scripture tells us that this world is under the influence of Satan, who is actively deceiving those who don't know God. The devil has his sights set on turning the next generation away from faith and the truth of God's Word. He would love nothing more than for us to be distracted from our God-given task of passing on faith.

First Peter 5:8 warns, "Be alert and of sober mind. Your enemy the devil prowls around like a roaring lion looking for someone to devour." The upcoming generations have a target on their backs. When I think back to my son's challenge to the Lord—"whoever gets me first"— I am deeply grateful that God stepped in. I trust that God answered my prayers and those of so many others when He took hold of Alvin's heart and life. I can't discount the influence and blessing of my great-grandfather, my grand-parents, and my parents in how everything worked out.

Another reason Generations is a timely message is because the allure of the world is strong. When I was growing up, worldliness was around. My parents only allowed us to listen to gospel music, fearing that the popular music of the day might have a negative influence on us. That concern seems mild compared to the influence the culture exerts today through the prevalence of the digital media and streaming entertainment. Surveys have shown that the average age a child receives a smartphone is ten years old, while 25 percent of kids under six have one.

Consider the words of 1 John 2:16: "For everything in the world—the lust of the flesh, the lust of the eyes, and the pride of life—comes not from the Father but from the world." God's way and the world's way are in direct opposition to one another. Many young people growing up today are being schooled in the ways of the world rather than the ways of God. The lust of the flesh and the eyes is accepted and even celebrated as we tell young people they deserve everything they want in life. Pride is rampant and seen in the arrogance, self-reliance, and spirit of offense that marks the world around us.

While observations like these can paint a picture of gloom and doom, I see many reasons for hope, and the existence of generations is one of them. God works through generations. Each one has its own unique way of expressing faith in God, and the Lord is faithful to every generation. The rising generation is meant to follow the faithful example of the generations who have gone before. This is God's design for the good of all people and for His glory.

Psalm 145:4–7 lays out a beautiful template for God's plan for the generations.

> One generation commends your works to another;
> they tell of your mighty acts.
> They speak of the glorious splendor of your
> majesty—
> and I will meditate on your wonderful works.
> They tell of the power of your awesome works—
> and I will proclaim your great deeds.
> They celebrate your abundant goodness
> and joyfully sing of your righteousness.

I love the verbs in this passage: they *commend*, they *tell*, they *speak*, they *meditate*, they *proclaim*, they *celebrate*, they *sing*. Yes, they sing! That takes me straight back to growing up in the Winans family. Not only did my parents proclaim God's wonderful works, but they also praised them and sang about them! Deuteronomy 6 talks of the many places we are to instruct our young people in God's precepts—along the road, sitting at home, when we lie down—and Psalm 145 tells us the many ways to say it.

Passing on faith to the next generation is meant to be a totally organic part of the Christian life—the outgrowth of a sincere and living faith. My hope is that by the end of this book, you will recognize how God has equipped you for this important task. I have discovered the deep joy that comes from joining Him in His pursuit of the next generation, and I want you to experience it too.

QUESTIONS *to* CONSIDER

- Who is someone in the older generation who has had an influence on you?

_____

_____

_____

_____

_____

- What is one way you can participate in passing down faith to the next generation?

_____

_____

_____

_____

_____

CHURCH IS NECESSARY

When I was growing up, about half of my waking hours were spent at church. On Sundays, the Winans family would arrive at church around 8:00 in the morning for Sunday school, which would be followed by a hearty breakfast of homemade biscuits, rice and gravy, eggs, and too many other delicious foods to mention. The mothers and grandmothers of the church prepared the feast, and I can still taste those biscuits melting in my mouth.

After breakfast, my whole family would attend Sunday morning service for two hours. Mom could sit us down in the front row and shoot us a look that dared us to move. No food was allowed in the sanctuary, and I still remember stern but kind ushers extending their white-gloved hands to relieve us of our chewing gum, which was also forbidden. We were taught from a young age to treat the house of the Lord with respect.

Pastor Jesse Stacks would preach the Word as my parents and other members of the congregation shouted, "Amen!" and "Yes, Lord!" As Pastor Stacks would be winding down his passionate message, the smell of homemade rolls, mac and cheese, collard greens, and sweet potatoes would waft through the air, causing our stomachs to growl and our mouths to water.

We'd file out of the morning service, greeting one another as we transitioned to enjoying Sunday dinner together. Along with the main dish, the counter would be filled with homemade cakes, pies, and even ice cream. When I became an adult, I realized how much work went into all that food. Most of us cook like this for Thanksgiving or Christmas, but these ladies prepared and brought a lavish feast every single Sunday!

After dinner, I'd go to Sunshine Band, our children's church, and my older brothers would head off to the programming for youth. Between band and the night service, the adults would visit while the kids ran and played outside or ran down to the corner store to buy penny candy. When 7:00 p.m. rolled around, we'd return to the main sanctuary for Sunday night service, which included worship, prayer, and another sermon. Many times, we wouldn't get home until after 10:00 p.m.

I'm sure few of us can imagine spending that amount of time in church today. Nowadays, folks start getting antsy and looking at their watches if the pastor preaches for more than thirty minutes. (I like to say that people are in a hurry to rush back to the struggle, because really, that's what awaits them.) But in those days, church was a one-stop shop where we received from God's Word and worshipped, but also where we ate, played, discussed the latest news, encouraged, worked, laughed, and *belonged.* I think Mom and Dad must have breathed a sigh of relief when the twelve of us stepped through that door of Mack Avenue Church of God in Christ on Sunday morning. They knew that an extended chosen family of aunts, uncles, and grandparents would be waiting to step in as surrogate caretakers of their brood.

Church wasn't just a marathon Sunday for us either. During the week we attended evening services on Tuesdays and Fridays, and choir rehearsals were on Saturday. There were always special events going on, such as revivals or shut-ins, where we stayed up all night praying and fasting. When I say we grew up in church, we *grew up* in church. That was the way of Pentecostal churches back then, and we loved it.

We all benefited from the community we found at Mack Avenue, the church my great-grandfather Winans had founded. Not only did we grow up with other Christian families by our side, we understood on a deep level that we were part of something bigger. Every generation was present, and each played a part in serving the body of Christ. From oldest to youngest, we all had a role; we all used our gifts. Pastor Stacks preached. The mothers and grandmothers made food. The men served as ministers and deacons. The young adults served as babysitters and role models. And the Winans sang.

Long before I was old enough to sing my first solo, my brothers were on that church platform singing. Our parents raised us to know that one of our primary purposes was to be a blessing to others and serve the church with our gifts. That's how I came to sing my first solo, "Fill My Cup, Lord," when I was eight years old. Sister Joyce Glenn, a relative and my Sunshine Band teacher, assigned me that solo. She believed I was ready, but I did not. I loved being in the Sunshine Band Choir, singing with all my friends. But the last thing I wanted was to be out front on that stage. I was very comfortable in the background. Singing that solo was never presented to me as an option, though. I *would* be singing it, whether I wanted to or not.

And so, at the church's annual convocation—a gathering of Pentecostal churches from around the region—I sang my debut solo. As I forced my feet to carry me from my seat in the audience to the microphone at the front of the church, my Mack Avenue family and actual family cheered me on: "Sing, CeCe!" "Sing, baby!" "Sing for Jesus, child."

I stepped up to the microphone, and Sister Glenn and I exchanged a look. Her warm smile gave me confidence, though I was still petrified. As the piano notes swelled, I began to sing.

Fill my cup, fill it up, and make me whole.

Tears streamed down my face during the entire performance, which I would reprise each year for many years after. I wish I could say I was overcome with emotion from the Holy Spirit, but the truth is, like Jonah in the Bible, I was a reluctant minister that day. Still, when I finished my song and saw those in the audience wiping their eyes, a warm feeling washed over me. I realized God had used me, and I felt His call to use my voice to minister within the church and beyond. Church had provided the context in which God showed me my purpose in His kingdom. At the tender age of eight, I discovered that

God could use me, CeCe Winans, to bless and encourage His people.

The beauty of the body of Christ is in that place, even a young child can be used by God. As we grew, my brothers, sisters, and I never doubted our purpose or value. Along with the blessing of loving, supportive parents, we were deeply rooted in a community of fellow believers who cheered us on in our race. I am reminded of the words found in Hebrews 12:1–2: "Therefore, since we are surrounded by such a great cloud of witnesses, let us throw off everything that hinders and the sin that so easily entangles. And let us run with perseverance the race marked out for us, fixing our eyes on Jesus, the pioneer and perfecter of faith."

The congregation at Mack Avenue was my cloud of witnesses. The fact is my own family made up an entire cheering section! When those saints encouraged me with "Sing, CeCe!" my dad was probably the loudest voice in the room. The sense of connection I had at church strengthened me for the challenges I faced as I headed into my teen years and adulthood. That community deeply shaped my values and desires. I was able to withstand peer pressure because I knew I wasn't alone. I had friends and fellow saints walking the same path and cheering me on, and I knew I'd see them again soon—and that we would have biscuits.

RESHAPING REALITY

I want to pause here to address those of you who have had a very different experience from mine. Maybe you didn't grow up attending church. Perhaps you've had a bad experience with the church and you're not currently attending. You may have read my story and thought, *That sounds a little too good to be true. What kid likes to go to church?* Or maybe you're wondering if I'm overselling it a bit. I urge you to hear me out. Jesus loves the church, and that's a good enough reason to consider, at the very least, how it could help us in this mission of passing on faith to the next generation.

One of the beautiful things about the body of Christ is that it offers an alternative to the world and the elements that shape us on a consistent basis. Our children are molded by what they hear at school, on television, from friends, in the locker room, and on the Internet. If you're like most American families, the time you spend at church is likely minimal compared to time given to these other influences. And yet, Romans 12:2 says clearly, "Do not conform to the pattern of this world, but be transformed by the renewing of your mind. Then you will be able to test and approve what God's will is—his good, pleasing and perfect will."

Church is a place where we engage in the process of having our minds renewed and our worldly thought patterns corrected. It's where we encourage one another and confess our sins. Church is the place where we experience the family of God—our brothers and sisters—reminding us of our shared purpose and God's wonderful works.

SECRET WEAPON

When our young family moved from Detroit to Nashville in 1989, one of Alvin's and my top priorities was finding a church to plug into. With two children ages five and under, we were looking for a church with a good children's ministry where we could also be fed spiritually and grow. We found that at Born Again Church, a nondenominational congregation. To me, church has always been an extended family. It's a place to put down roots and watch things grow. Alvin III and Ashley were both baptized there as teenagers.

We attended church as a family on Sunday morning and for Wednesday Bible study. My children understood

Church is the place
where we experience
the family of God—our
brothers and sisters—
reminding us of our
shared purpose and
God's wonderful works.

church was not optional. But I believe they were happy and truly enjoyed being there. Church was a safe place, a shelter from the world, where they heard the Word of God and came to saving faith in Christ. Our church attendance wasn't perfect, but it was an integral part of our week and identity as a family.

Because in my family attending church was nonnegotiable, honoring the Lord and going to church were inseparable. Our involvement with our local church was central, and everything else went around it. Today I observe the opposite: we have our lives and activities ("the struggle"), and we squeeze God in where we can. Sports, travel, and recreation compete for our allegiance to the church.

Polls show that just about 35 percent of American families attend religious services on a regular basis, with only 20 percent attending weekly.[1] (And these statistics came before the worldwide pandemic that further curtailed church attendance.) To me, this consistent decline in church attendance we've seen over the past fifty years is a sign that we may not be effectively passing on faith.

---

1. "Just How Religious Are Americans?," The Austin Institute for the Study of Family and Culture, accessed June 20, 2022, https://relationshipsinamerica.com/religion/just-how-religious -are-americans.

And yet, the gathering of the faithful is what God uses to transfer faith from one generation to the next; I believe the local church is one of the most underutilized tools for passing on faith to the next generation. In Old Testament times, this work was accomplished through the spiritual rituals and services at the tabernacle and in the synagogue. The people spent hours each week with their faith communities, reminding one another of God's statutes and His promise to send a Messiah. In this context, they taught their children about the Lord and how they were to follow Him.

Gathering with the fellowship of believers continued to be a practice in the New Testament. Jesus founded the church on His disciple Peter "the Rock." This is how Peter describes the church: "You are a chosen people, a royal priesthood, a holy nation, God's special possession, that you may declare the praises of him who called you out of darkness into his wonderful light. Once you were not a people, but now you are the people of God; once you had not received mercy, but now you have received mercy" (1 Peter 2:9–10).

Through the church, Jesus made us "a people," His special possession, diverse but united in Christ. The apostle Paul spent much of the epistles affirming the importance of the church and describing its function. Perhaps one of the most compelling pictures of the church he provides is the bride of Christ: "Husbands, love your wives, just as Christ loved the church and gave himself up for her to make her holy, cleansing her by the washing with water through the word, and to present her to himself as a radiant church, without stain or wrinkle or any other blemish, but holy and blameless" (Ephesians 5:25–27).

What a beautiful, personal picture of Christ's covenant love for the true believers who comprise His church. On my wedding day, I wore a beautiful white dress and veil. As I walked down that aisle, all eyes were on me. But the eyes that mattered most were those of my adoring groom, Alvin. The love a bride feels on her wedding day is second to none. That is the love Christ has for the church.

As I have counseled through the years, I have encountered many stories of people being hurt and misunderstood by the church. Hearing about some of these sad experiences, I understand how the enemy could entice some to abandon the church altogether. I am grieved by it, and I believe our Lord Jesus weeps over the mistreatment of His beloved and how these incidents misrepresent Him. Leaving the church will not solve our problems; it will only compound them. If you have been hurt by the church, I am sorry and would suggest that you grieve that.

But we cannot deny the fact that the church—true believers around the world—is still the bride of Christ, honored and adored. And He desires to wash her in His Word and present her as a blameless, radiant bride. Look to Jesus for healing and redemption, and pray that He would lead you to a congregation that is faithfully preaching and practicing His Word.

When it comes to passing on faith to the next generation, I believe church is not only a necessary ingredient but also a secret weapon. As I've reflected on my own church experiences and those I desire for my children and grandchildren, here are a few benefits I see of filling those pews.

Church offers a rich, multigenerational experience with fellow believers. When I walked through the doors of Mack Avenue, I encountered saints of all ages. I had a front-row seat to watching mature believers working out their salvation, serving, loving, giving, testifying, and walking in the Spirit. I observed my parents honoring and respecting their elders. I witnessed the older women pouring into the younger women. The teenagers and young adults looked up to my mom and dad and served them by helping with their youngsters.

When people in the church had needs, I watched as those in the congregation rallied to help. They worked willingly without expecting anything in return. They simply served as Scripture commands, gladly with joyful hearts. I imagine this was like the early church, where "all the believers were together and had everything in common" (Acts 2:44). Young and old worshipped together and cared for each other in a way that resembled a family. In my experience, church *is* a family. Having everything in common didn't mean they were a homogenous congregation. In actuality, the early church was a diverse group of Greeks, Jews, and other ethnicities, all united by salvation through Jesus. Christians of all ages and backgrounds benefited from the mutual edification of coming together.

Church reinforces the precepts of God. One of the purposes of the local church is to teach and protect sound doctrine. So much of my life centered around God's Word simply because I was always sitting in those pews. There were times when the Winans kids nodded off or sat in the back finishing a homework assignment, but my mom didn't mind. She figured the Word was working its way into our hearts and doing its good work there.

"I don't care if you fall asleep," she'd say. "At least you're in the atmosphere. Things are going in your mind that you don't even know are going in." And she was right. Over time, soaking in "the atmosphere" transformed me.

Church was where I memorized Scripture, received biblical teaching, and learned what God required of me as His follower. I may not have been listening to the Word all the time, but I was constantly hearing it.

I've adopted this philosophy with my toddler grandson, Wyatt. I often read Scripture out loud to him, and we listen to verses set to music. I tell him, "You are a mighty man of God." Although he doesn't understand much of it yet, he is learning that his family believes in God and follows Him.

I am so thankful for the foundation I received. Had I not spent all those hours in church, flipping open the pages of my old King James Version Bible and taking notes in my worn notebook, I would not be the woman of the Word God steadily transformed me into. Church offers our children the benefit of other voices reaching them with the truth of God's Word and reinforcing what they've heard in the home.

Church provides a context to live out our calling. Another benefit of church involvement is that it reminds us of our unique calling as Christians. The Greek word *ekklesia,* from which we get the New Testament word *church,* means "a called-out assembly or congregation." The church is a gathering that instructs us how to live biblically and provides a context for doing so.

Every day the world tells us what is best for our children, and this information is not always in line with what we find in Scripture. The world encourages us to give our children opportunities for academic and athletic advancement; raise them to respect different points of view and treat others with kindness; and instill in them the character and self-control to steer clear of drugs, alcohol, and other destructive influences.

While these are all positive things, statistics show that our best efforts are falling short when it comes to raising happy, healthy adults. Cases of anxiety and depression among youth are on the rise, nearly doubling during the pandemic.[2] Despite having an abundance of opportunities and activities, many teens describe feeling a lack of purpose in their lives. I am not at all saying that teens who attend church will not experience the struggles that plague their peers; they may. However, being immersed in a healthy church family provides a sense of purpose and community.

---

2. N. Racine, B. A. McArthur, J. E. Cooke, R. Eirich, J. Zhu, and S. Madigan. "Global Prevalence of Depressive and Anxiety Symptoms in Children and Adolescents During COVID-19: A Meta-analysis." *JAMA Pediatrics* 175, no. 11 (2021): 1142–1150, https://doi.org/10.1001/jamapediatrics.2021.2482.

For my mom and dad, church was a place that reinforced the calling they found in Scripture and were seeking to pass down to their children. Growing up at Mack Avenue Church and later Shalom Temple, I never questioned that I had a purpose and a calling. From the moment I sang that first solo for Sister Glenn, I knew God could use me. I didn't know exactly what my future held, but I knew my true purpose in life was to love God and spread that love to others.

As I grew, I discovered the gifts God had given me—obviously ministering through music but also gifts of teaching and exhortation. I'm not sure I would have discovered these competencies apart from the context of the local church. Scripture depicts the church as body parts contributing to the healthy performance of one body. I love that vivid picture. The members can never do individually what they can do together. And the healthiest churches are those where each part is functioning in the job it was designed to do supported by all the other parts.

Church provides a sense of belonging. One of the greatest benefits I have gained from the body of Christ is the comfort of belonging. For the past four decades, I have traveled all over the world. Each place I go, I find home with fellow believers in the church. My siblings and I never minded going to church as kids because our friends were there. At school I may have been called a "holy roller," but within the walls of my church I was valued, seen, and loved. I had many role models apart from my parents and siblings who poured into me and helped strengthen my faith.

A well-known African proverb says, "It takes a village to raise a child." This was very true of my childhood church experiences. Within its walls, my parents found a community ready and willing to reinforce the faith they were teaching us in the home. My spiritual wellness and moral upbringing were a concern to everyone, not just my parents. The people of my home church were my extended family, and I valued their input into my life.

NECESSARY, NOT OPTIONAL

Not long ago, I was on the show *Better Together* with author and speaker Amie Dockery, and she said something profound: "What we make optional, the next generation will deem unnecessary." Whew. Oh Lord, let that sink in. When we see ungodliness or irreverence for God's house in the upcoming generation, we must consider if part of that is a result of us making church optional. The next natural step is for them to believe that church must not be that important and that it might even be unnecessary. Yet when you look at what our young people are up against, they need Jesus and His church more than ever.

We need to wake up and consider whether we're placing our children into an environment that will lead to deeper faith. I have spoken with many parents and grandparents whose desire is to see their young people come to saving faith in Christ and flourish in their spiritual walks. However, some of them are leaving out this significant piece—making church a priority for their families.

When I think back to those marathon Sundays at Mack Avenue, I hold many fond memories. Those days may be distant, but I can remember the sweetness, love, and community they held. Psalm 34:8 says, "Taste and see that the LORD is good; blessed is the one who takes refuge in him." For me, church has been a refuge from the world and a place where I can live out my calling and be my true self. It has been a place where I have tasted and seen God's goodness (and feasted on some of the best *actual* meals of my life). That is what church was meant to be.

When Alvin and I founded Nashville Life, I wanted to help create a similarly inviting atmosphere where young people would be drawn in. I hoped to replicate the best of what I received in those formative years at Mack Avenue and Shalom Temple. I hope we all proclaim with David, "I rejoiced with those who said to me, 'Let us go to the house of the LORD' " (Psalm 122:1). If we want to pass on vibrant faith to the next generation, we need to help them experience the power and community of the local church. Church is not optional; it is necessary.

- What is your church background? How does that affect your current relationship with it?

  _____

  _____

  _____

- What are some ways the local church has influenced you or strengthened your faith?

  _____

  _____

  _____

- What evidence does Scripture offer that the church is to be a vital part of the Christian life?

  _____

  _____

  _____

three

YOU'VE ALREADY GOT IT

When I was seventeen years old, my brother BeBe and I got on an airplane and flew to the location of our first full-time singing gig on a Christian television program. I still can't believe my parents allowed us—especially me— to go. My father wouldn't allow me to stay around the corner, so allowing me to move to another city seemed unlikely. I had just graduated from high school and was so inexperienced. I had never even worn makeup! But my parents were confident in how they had raised us and knew their children would look out for one another. It turns out, their faith in BeBe and me was well placed.

Ever since my first solo when I was eight, I had taken the stage many times. I continued singing in the church and in youth choirs, where I sometimes directed.

And the Winans family put on yearly Mother's Day and Christmas concerts to bless the community. As many times as I had stepped onto that stage, I still felt a bit uncomfortable. I loved to fade into the background, and performing forced me to be front and center. By that time, four of my older brothers—Ronald, Marvin, Carvin, and Michael—had formed The Testimonial Singers (who later changed their name to The Winans). They performed in Detroit and the surrounding areas until they were discovered by California gospel legend Andraé Crouch; then their careers exploded. At home in Detroit, I watched with pride as my older brothers' music took them to new heights. In 1981, they signed their first recording contract and began touring the nation singing gospel music. God had answered my great-grandfather's prophecy that the Winans children would spread God's Word through singing!

When BeBe and I began our journey of singing together, I hardly felt qualified. What did a seventeen-year-old girl have to say about faith and walking with Jesus? And who would listen? But as I performed in the singing group on the show, people did listen. To my amazement, our audiences not only seemed to be moved by the songs I sang, but they also identified with my message of hope in Christ.

I still had shy tendencies, but the more I ministered from the stage, the more I recognized God was using me and I did have something to say. While part of me wanted to stay safely tucked away in Detroit, allowing my older siblings to fulfill the destiny my great-grandfather had prayed over us, another side of me had been awakened. I wanted to give God all of me so that He could take the gift that He had given me as far as He wanted to.

WHAT'S IN YOUR HOUSE?

There's a fascinating story in 2 Kings 4 about a single mother in crisis. Her deceased husband had been part of a company of prophets that hung out with the prophet Elisha. The woman came to Elisha in dire straits. "Your servant my husband is dead," she said; "and you know that he revered the LORD. But now his creditor is coming to take my two boys as his slaves." Reading the story, you can feel the woman's hopelessness. In fact, she appeals to the great man of God because she needs rescue from the seemingly inevitable tragedy ahead.

In a God-helps-those-who-help-themselves moment, the prophet replies, "How can I help you? Tell me, what do you have in your house?" Have you ever felt this challenge from the Lord? "What do you have in your house?

What resources have I already provided?" I'm sure Elisha could have just asked God to change the widow's circumstances without her involvement, but he turned the situation on her and asked what she had in her house to solve the dilemma.

The woman responded as I think many of us would. "Your servant has nothing there at all," but that wasn't quite true. Because as she's picturing her home with its everyday necessities, she continues, "Except a small jar of olive oil." It's no wonder the little she had didn't seem like a viable solution to the woman. How could a small jar of olive oil possibly solve her problems?

As we consider the task of passing on faith to the next generation in a moment in time when so much of the culture around us goes against the Bible and God's ways, we can easily feel that we have nothing to offer. When the news headlines shout of the evil in our world, we cry, "Lord, have mercy" and "Jesus come quickly," realizing that He is the only hope for this dark world. Putting our faith in Him is essential, but we should also ask, "What do I have in my house? What are the gifts God has already provided so that I can accomplish this vital, God-given mission of telling the generations about who God is and what He has done?"

Once the widow had revealed that she had a small jar of olive oil, the prophet sprang into action, helping her come up with a plan. He told her to go to all her neighbors and borrow as many jars and containers as she could gather. "Don't ask for just a few," he exhorted. She was to be bold in asking for as many vessels as she possibly could. Next, he instructed her to take all the containers into her house and close the door. She would then pour the oil from her small jar into all the vessels she had collected.

As she began to pour, the oil from her small jar filled each container her sons had brought her until none remained. I like to think about what might have happened if she and her sons had collected even more jars! How many times do we underestimate what God can and will do with our meager offerings? I'm sure as the woman poured the oil and filled jar after jar, her confidence grew and her doubts shrank. As she engaged in the miracle God was doing, she got to witness firsthand how God could turn something very small into something great.

When she had filled the final jar, she asked her son to bring her another. "There is not a jar left," he replied. And when he said those words, the oil stopped flowing. I think it's telling that the widow had become unaware of how many jars were left. As she continued to pour the oil, her faith grew that it would keep flowing no matter how many jars she filled. The work was not cumbersome because she was experiencing a small taste of God's unlimited resources.

She returned to Elisha and told him what had happened. He said, "Go, sell the oil and pay your debts. You and your sons can live on what is left." God's provision for the woman was not only for her present circumstances. He had provided her enough to live on, presumably until her sons were old enough to provide for the family.

I love that the woman included her sons in the process. She gave them the opportunity to participate and feel invested. Along with their mother, I imagine they were also expectant to see how God would use their obedience. Imagine how their faith must have exploded as they watched God do a miracle for them.

DIFFERENT AGE, SAME PROBLEMS

I have talked to many people who do not feel up to the task of planting faith in the next generation. "Is it even possible?" they ask. Looking at the issue through a strictly human lens, the task does seem daunting. The cultural landscape is far from hospitable for such an assignment. Our world seems to be in a state of confusion and chaos and getting worse every day. When I think about what I dealt with in high school versus what today's youth encounters, the difference is staggering.

My parents' greatest concerns were that one of us would be pulled into a "bad crowd" and away from Christ. They did all they could to strengthen us in a holy lifestyle so that our heads and hearts wouldn't be turned by the ways of the world. But they didn't have to contend with cell phones and the Internet and the rampant debauchery being broadcasted on TV and social media outlets. My goodness, sometimes I wonder what my dear Grandmother Howze would have to say about such things!

Looking at the degradation surrounding us, it's easy to feel hopeless, like the widow who came to Elisha. She wanted to provide for her sons and rescue them from physical slavery, while many of us want to nourish the next generation with God's truth and rescue them from the sins that cause a person to lose their soul. But we find in Scripture many examples of God's people passing on faith in the context of hostile environments. Here are just a few examples:

- Jonah reluctantly proclaimed God's judgment to the morally bankrupt and perverse Assyrian city of Nineveh, and the whole city repented and was saved.
- Daniel, a Jew exiled in Babylon, continued to follow God in a pagan culture, which ultimately affected the people around him and inspired kings to praise the Hebrew God.
- The apostle Paul spread the gospel and built up the church in Rome, even as the depraved, violent leader Nero Claudius Caesar was propagating and carrying out the brutal persecution of Christians.

We may be tempted to feel as if our world has special, insurmountable problems. But Scripture reveals that God's people have always been following Him and doing His work in inhospitable places and times. Every age has its own set of philosophies, values, and social norms that influence the culture. Ephesians 2:1–2 puts it like this: "As for you, you were dead in your transgressions and sins, in which you used to live when you followed the ways of this world and of the ruler of the kingdom of the air, the spirit who is now at work in those who are disobedient."

Like a flowing river, the course of this world can be difficult to resist. As believers, we are called to swim upstream, not go with the flow of the world. Apart from the power of Christ in us, this is a wearying proposition. The world does not make it easy to live a life of faith. In fact, we can't expect the world to support Christ's agenda. But when we consider what the Lord did through Jonah, Daniel, and Paul, it's easy to see that the inhospitable environment had little to do with the end result.

At first glance, we may look at our circumstances, our resources, our stations in life, or our personalities, and say, like the widow in 2 Kings, "There is nothing there at all!" We may feel we possess nothing that will help us carry out · this mission of passing on faith to the next generation. But God sees things differently. He asks, "What's in your house? What have I already provided for you to carry out the calling?"

The truth is, God has made us for this. Over and over in Scripture, He instructs us to teach our children His precepts and model how to live a life of faith. And the one who calls you is faithful. Second Peter 1:3 gives us this promise: "His divine power has given us everything we need for a godly life through our knowledge of him who called us by his own glory and goodness." The message of that verse is clear: God's power gives us everything we need to live out His calling for our lives.

THREE LIES THE ENEMY TELLS

Even though Scripture is clear that we have "everything we need" to accomplish God's good plans for us, the enemy carries on an active campaign to convince us otherwise. When I was seventeen and God was calling me into music ministry, you can be sure the enemy was whispering the lies in my ear that I wasn't up to such a task. I wish I could say, many years later, that I'm immune to the deceptions of the enemy, but combatting his lies with God's truth will be a lifelong endeavor.

Speaking of Satan in John 8:44, Jesus says, "When he lies, he speaks his native language, for he is a liar and the father of lies." If the enemy had a resume, lying would be included under "special skills." He's not just good at it, it is his *native language*, his go-to form of communication. Think about the serpent in the garden, who told Eve and her husband, Adam, that their disobedience would not lead to death but would, in fact, cause them to be like God. The lie worked like a charm on our first ancestors, and they will work on us if we are not constantly opposing the lies with truth.

Here are three lies the enemy tells us about passing on faith.

The task is too difficult. As we've already discussed, when we look at the world around us, the goal of establishing the next generation in a strong, biblical faith can seem impossible. When we look at our world and see how ungodliness and unbelief is running rampant, we may feel like real change is unattainable. As the numbers of young people leaving the faith and leaving the church grow, we can begin to focus on the problem and forget about our powerful God.

Like Peter, who believed he could walk on water, saw the waves, and began to sink, our sense of purpose and calling can be muted as we see the waves of depression, anxiety, anger, addiction, violence, sexual brokenness, and so much more washing over our young people. We can feel helpless to stop the onslaught of false ideology that engulfs them and push back the darkness.

I have observed parents pulling back from teaching and guiding their teenagers just when they should be pressing in. We the church must be careful not to fail to invest in young adults just because it doesn't get the return or buy-in that ministry to other groups garners. I've seen grandparents accept passive roles in the lives of their grandchildren because they don't believe their influence makes a difference. Viewing the struggles the average child, teenager, or young adult faces today, it's easy to feel as if the task is too big or it's too late for God to redeem the next generation.

But that is a lie. Psalm 100:5 says, "For the LORD is good and his love endures forever; his faithfulness continues through all generations." When we're tempted to give up on the next generation and declare the task of reaching them too difficult, we ignore the fact that God is faithful to *every* generation. When the waves of doubt pull us away from our calling, we must turn our eyes to Jesus, recognizing that it is His power through us that accomplishes things the world says are impossible.

You're not qualified. One of the biggest lies of the enemy is that we are not qualified to do God's work. When Alvin and I founded Nashville Life Church, we did not feel qualified. In fact, for more than a decade, it was hard for us to believe God was calling us to pastor a church. While I had finally settled into my role as a singer and minister of the gospel in that arena, becoming a pastor for a church was a whole other matter. The idea of teaching for an extended period and mentoring impressionable young men and women was sobering. I felt the weight of that responsibility (as I should have).

One of the biggest
lies of the enemy is that
we are not qualified
to do God's work.

Satan is an accuser, and he loves to remind us of our deficits. Have you ever said, "Oh, I could never do that"? I have. And yet Scripture tells us all things are possible with God. There was a time when I didn't think I could stand on a stage alone for five minutes, let alone teach for an hour! But I read in the Bible that I am an approved worker who can correctly handle God's Word (2 Timothy 2:15).

Another way the enemy lies to us is by rubbing our noses in our failures. We may feel disqualified from ministering to the next generation because of past sin. Let me just say, if sin disqualified us from doing the work of God, no one would be doing it. The Bible is full of imperfect people and parents. Rebekah favored her younger son, Jacob, and plotted with him to deceive his father, Isaac. Jacob, repeating his mother's sin, favored his son Joseph, creating division among his children. And King David, described as a man after God's own heart, was an absentee, passive father who raised rebellious sons who perpetuated evil. Each of these imperfect parents had faith in God and still played a role in passing down faith to the next generation, reminding us that God works through flawed people.

Maybe as you're reading these words, you feel shame over your failures, either as a parent or in another area of life. Let me remind you that shame does not come from God. Jesus paid the price to take away our shame when He died on Calvary. Now we can stand blameless before a holy and righteous God. First John 1:9 says, "If we confess our sins, he is faithful and just and will forgive us our sins and purify us from all unrighteousness." If you are a true believer in Jesus, you are not disqualified. In fact, it's just the opposite. God has given you everything you need to pass on faith to the next generation.

Somebody else can do it better. Similar to the last lie, this one convinces you that someone else is *more* qualified than you—the youth pastor, the Sunday school teacher, the gifted speaker. Something I have noticed is that many parents seek to outsource the spiritual training and development of their children and teenagers. They bring their young people to Sunday school, church, and youth group in the hopes that they will believe in Jesus and grow in their faith.

There's nothing wrong with taking your kids to church (You already know how I feel about that). These programs can be wonderful reinforcers of the spiritual training happening in the home. But the belief that a pastor or youth leader is more qualified to pass on faith to your child than you, the parent, is a lie. Research confirms that parents, and especially moms, are the biggest influence on their children's spiritual journey and decision to follow Jesus.[3] Children who grow up in homes with one or two believing parents are exponentially more likely to claim to have faith in Christ as adults. This is encouraging news! God truly has given parents the most defining role in their children's spiritual development.

THREE GIFTS WE ALREADY POSSESS

Now that we have identified the lies that may be keeping us from getting on board with reaching the next generation for Christ, it's time to consider what's "in our house." What has God already provided to help us carry out this calling? James 1:17 encourages us with these words: "Every good and perfect gift is from above, coming down from the Father of the heavenly lights, who does not change like shifting shadows." The Lord gives us perfect gifts as we walk in faith and live out the things to which He's called us. While it would be easy to come up with a very long list, here are three gifts each of us possess.

---

3. Dale Hudson, "How Parents Affect Their Children's Faith (the Latest Findings)," ChurchLeaders.com, December 27, 2018, https://churchleaders.com/children/childrens-ministry -articles/296226-parents-affect-childrens-faith-latest-findings .html.

Salvation. Every person who has professed faith in Jesus Christ and His redemptive work on the cross receives God's most precious gift. When we admit our sin and trust in Jesus, who died and rose again, as our Savior and Lord, God immediately bestows on us the gift of salvation and eternal life through Him. Ephesians 2:8 says, "For it is by grace you have been saved, through faith—and this is not from yourselves, it is the gift of God." Because of this gift we are transferred from death to life and brought into God's glorious kingdom. From that moment on, we can tell others the Good News of the gospel. We don't have to have a theology degree or be a pastor. The minute we decide to repent of our sin and to follow Jesus, we are qualified to tell others about the transformation we have experienced.

A personal testimony. Each of us has a unique testimony of how we came to Christ and how He has transformed our lives. Some come to know the Lord quietly as children, while others are rescued by Him in dramatic fashion. My own testimony was a combination. When I was growing up, pastors preached about hell . . . a lot. So I asked Jesus into my heart multiple times, just to be sure I was heaven bound. I began to sense the Spirit's presence in my life when I was very young. Around eight years old, I made a personal decision to follow Jesus, and I never looked back. I used to wonder if my testimony was exciting enough to draw others to a relationship with Christ. But I've come to realize that God has used my quiet testimony of His faithfulness throughout my life to show others the beauty of walking with Him for many years. The wholeness He preserved in me from a young age has centered me and given me strength as I minister to others.

Perhaps your testimony is more dramatic than mine. Praise the Lord! God can use any story; they all have power because He is the author. Revelation 12:10–11 says, "For the accuser of our brothers and sisters, who accuses them before our God, day and night, has been hurled down. They triumphed over him by the blood of the Lamb and by the word of their testimony." Testimonies are powerful! And you have one. And the best part is, you don't have to be a great evangelist or orator to tell someone your story.

Spiritual gifts. Scripture tells us that when we become a Christian, we receive spiritual gifts. These competencies are distinct from our natural abilities and are given at the time of salvation. Listen to what the apostle Paul tells us about these gifts:

> We have different gifts, according to the grace given to each of us. If your gift is prophesying, then prophesy in accordance with your faith; if it is serving, then serve; if it is teaching, then teach;

if it is to encourage, then give encouragement; if
it is giving, then give generously; if it is to lead, do
it diligently; if it is to show mercy, do it cheerfully.
(Romans 12:6–8)

This is one of three passages in Scripture that provide a list of spiritual gifts. (Two other lists appear in 1
Corinthians 12:4–11 and 1 Corinthians 12:28.) But this
passage reveals two important principles. The first is that
we have different gifts. No two Christians are the same.
While we are all equipped for good works, we possess
individual, God-given traits that help us accomplish those
good works. Just as the widow didn't think much of her
jar of oil, we may be tempted to view our gifts as insignificant. We may even compare them to someone else's. But
that is foolish. God has given us the exact gifts He knows
we need for the calling.

The second principle found in Romans 12 is God
expects us to use our gifts. I've always loved the children's
gospel song "This Little Light of Mine." As a child, I especially relished the part where we sang, "Hide it under a
bushel—no! I'm gonna let it shine." God does not intend
for our gifts to lie dormant or stay hidden. He made them
to shine. As we use our spiritual gifts, we build up the
church, edifying the believers and reaching the lost.

The good news about spiritual gifts is that they have nothing to do with our talent or lack of it. I may have been born with the natural ability to sing, but that is not my spiritual gift. When I received Jesus as my Savior, the Holy Spirit bestowed on me the gifts of teaching and encouragement. If you are a Christ-follower, you also have spiritual gifts. You may already have identified those gifts. If not, you won't have to look far to find a quiz online or in a book that can help you discover what those gifts are so you can start using them.

GETTING STARTED

Years ago, I couldn't imagine where the Lord would take me or how He would use my ministry to touch others. When I was that shy seventeen-year-old singing songs on the *Praise the Lord* show, I had no idea what the years ahead held: A record contract and successful singing career as "BeBe and CeCe" followed by a solo career. Meeting and marrying my husband, Alvin. Becoming close, deep friends with Whitney Houston. Raising a son and daughter. Singing for celebrities and presidents. Burying a brother and my father. Winning prestigious awards. Founding a church. Becoming a grandmother.

My life so far has been quite the mix of sparkly, public successes and unseen, holy moments. Like the widow of 2 Kings, I brought my small jar of oil, not sure it would amount to much, and God did the rest. With each opportunity, big or small, the Lord gave me exactly what I needed. And over time, I realized that God *had* given me something worth sharing—Himself. He had equipped me with everything I needed to proclaim His name to the next generation. All I had to do was be faithful to pour the oil into the containers He provided.

- Think about your own story so far. What have been some of the highs and lows you've experienced, both public and private?

_____

_____

_____

- What do you already possess that God could use to spread His name and fame to the next generation?

_____

_____

_____

- How can He use your story and gifts to manifest His presence in the lives of others and fill them with the reality of His love?

_____

_____

_____

four

PUTTING IN THE WORK

I wouldn't say growing up in the Winans household was like bootcamp, but my parents definitely ran a tight ship. For my first four years of life, I was the only girl among seven older brothers. You can imagine the chaos created by seven young men living in cramped quarters. Fights rarely broke out under the watchful eyes of my parents, but when they were out of the house, all bets were off.

As for my place in the pack, my brothers say I was spoiled, but my mother says I was just "good." As a quiet and compliant child, my demeanor provided quite a contrast to my spirited older brothers, who were always challenging each other and getting into some kind of mischief or another. Although I required fewer consequences, I still found ways to test the boundaries. One time, I engaged in a water fight with my brothers just after I'd received a hard press style at the beauty shop. That style, popular for little black girls at the time, was supposed to keep my locks smooth and straight for two weeks. But the water caused my hair to frizz, and my brothers and I received quite the whipping when my mom returned home.

When my parents were home, order reigned. They both believed discipline was a virtue. And when we strayed from acceptable behavior, there were consequences. Mom and Pop Winans lived by the words of Proverbs 13:24: "Whoever spares the rod hates their children, but the one who loves their children is careful to discipline them."

While we have different opinions on "spare the rod, spoil the child," I think we all can appreciate the second part of that verse: "The one who loves their children is careful to discipline them." This was very much my parents' perspective. They carefully disciplined us because they loved us—even if my siblings and I sometimes wished they would be less careful.

I wrote this in my memoir, *On a Positive Note*: "Above all, 'home training' meant respecting your parents, respecting elders, no talking back, and having a fear of God. I learned a large part of what it means to be a parent from watching my parents teach us discipline and respect."[1]

LIFE LESSONS

Parenting in this way required a lot of effort and intentionality. My mom would work all day as a medical transcriptionist at a local hospital and then come home to train and nurture her brood. She would have conversations with us, sew many of our outfits, and help us prepare for school the next day. As a parent myself, I recognize how easy it is to let little character flaws and behavior problems go uncorrected. Applying careful discipline isn't a joyride. But here's why it matters. When we discipline our children, we model the character of God.

Proverbs 3:12 tells us, "The LORD disciplines those he loves, as a father the son he delights in." Correction is an act of love. The parent who disciplines this way has his or her child's best at heart. I was fortunate to feel this love in my parents' discipline. They would tell me the truth about my sin and make sure I felt the weight of its

---

1. CeCe Winans, *On a Positive Note: Her Joyous Faith, Her Life in Music, and Her Everyday Blessings* (New York: Pocket Books, 1999), 14.

consequences, but later there would be an embrace and reassurance that everything was OK. They didn't hold grudges, and I never doubted they loved me.

Looking back, I can see they disciplined us to protect us from consequences we could face later in life if we did not develop prudence and self-control. Even at the time, we had more rules than the average family. Those rules outlawed dancing, parties, makeup, sleepovers, and going to movies. Though my mom and dad set strict parameters, they were fair. They heard us out if we brought them a request, and they were wise and judicious.

Along with providing discipline, my parents took us to church on a regular basis. We could be found in those pews three days a week. As I've already mentioned, taking in the Word of God and Christian fellowship had a profound influence on us. It's true that you become like those you run with. I know it was a big commitment for my mom and dad to get ten children up and ready for church each Sunday morning. They may have had other activities they would have liked to pursue during the week, other than taking us to multiple church meetings. But if they did, we never heard about it. Being part of Christian community was a priority for our family.

One of my favorite things about my home was the godly, grace-filled atmosphere and the sense of safety.

We would gather around the piano in our small living room and sing one song after another for hours on end. I remember my parents and grandparents discussing the Scriptures with us in an informal and authentic way. One thing I didn't sense was a formula. We didn't do a certain number of family Bible studies per week or eat dinner together every night. My parents' jobs and our activities didn't always allow for that. But God was a natural part of our home, our ultimate authority and a topic that came up regularly.

Each day before we left for school, my mom would pray with us, commissioning us to live for Christ in whatever challenges we would face that day. I imagine those prayers protected us from many of the devil's schemes and gave us the boldness we needed to live differently from our peers. I already looked different with my long skirts and makeup-free face, and those morning prayers reminded me of why I lived by a different standard. I saw how prayer could change my daily circumstances and help me when I faced challenges.

As I think back to my childhood, my parents' investment in my spiritual life was massive. They both worked full-time jobs, but our upbringing was as important to them as their work outside the home. It was more important, in fact. They put in the work. Their method of instilling faith in their children wasn't groundbreaking or complicated, but it was labor intensive. It was made up of many daily decisions that supported their overall objective of raising us to fear the Lord. They knew their goal, and they were willing to take the steps necessary to reach it.

PLANTING POWERFUL FAITH

Maybe as you read the description of my childhood "home training," you found yourself feeling a little exhausted. Me too! My parents, and many in their generation, excelled at working hard to pass on faith to the next generation. (Part of that could be they just worked harder at things in general.) My parents made sure we were grounded in the Word and immersed in Christian community. They had their flaws, of course, but their strength was diligently teaching their children about God through every aspect of life. They showed us what it looks like to love God with your whole heart, not bending to what the world says is good.

The Bible tells us that a person reaps what they sow. They harvest what they plant. Galatians 6:8 explains this concept well: "Whoever sows to please their flesh, from the flesh will reap destruction; whoever sows to please the Spirit, from the spirit will reap eternal life." I don't know about you, but I sure do feel the world's pull to sow to please the flesh. How often do we hear these phrases?

"Treat yourself."

"Pamper yourself; you deserve it."

"Take care of you."

It is so easy to see self-care as the top priority. Believe me. I get it. Overall, we're a busy, burned-out bunch, aren't we? In fact, studies show that one in fourteen children in the United States has a caregiver with poor mental health.[2] Many of us are running on fumes. Some of us find ourselves at a breaking point. Like being on an airplane with a child, you need to put that oxygen mask on yourself before you can help someone else.

Please hear my heart. You may need a break, and that's OK. Take the break. Find support. Allow God to refresh you. But *then* be about the work of sowing faith into the next generation. Say I wanted fresh tomatoes in my vegetable garden, then I would need to plant tomato seeds. I can choose to plant peas instead, but when that plant grows, it won't yield juicy, red tomatoes. The same is true of tending the faith of the younger generation. If we want

---

2. "Mental Health of Children and Parents—a Strong Connection," Centers for Disease Control and Prevention, April 19, 2022, www.cdc.gov/childrensmentalhealth/features /mental-health-children-and-parents.html.

to instill faith and godliness into our children and grand-children, we must plant those seeds through our daily actions. We must read the Scripture and have conversations about it. We must talk about what God is doing in our lives. We must pray with our children and over them. We must model for them how we trust the Lord through trials. We must teach them to love their enemies. This is sowing to the Spirit, and it bears good fruit.

If we use our time differently—binge-watching our favorite TV shows, mindlessly scrolling through social media, indulging fear and worry, working incessantly, outsourcing our children's spiritual training to the church only—we will produce a different crop. I am not trying to lay a guilt trip; no parent or family will be perfect. But we have to know our goal and stick to a plan that will accomplish that goal. This process of planting faith in our children doesn't have to be elaborate, but it does require work.

As I look at my rich Christian heritage and what God has taught me as a mother and grandmother, here are a few ways I believe we can plant seeds of faith in our children.

Teach them the Word of God. This sounds deceptively simple. But going back to Deuteronomy 6 we can see it takes consistency and effort to pass on the precepts of the

If we want to instill
faith and godliness
into our children and
grandchildren, we must
plant those seeds through
our daily actions.

Lord. Let's revisit that passage: "These commandments that I give you today are to be on your hearts. Impress them on your children. Talk about them when you sit at home and when you walk along the road, when you lie down and when you get up. Tie them as symbols on your hands and bind them on your foreheads" (Galatians 6:6–8).

This passage instructs the people to teach their children God's precepts throughout the day everywhere they go. And verse 6 provides the key: God's instructions for life are to be on *our hearts* as the older generation. Our excitement for God's Word will naturally overflow into conversations with our young people.

The reality is that right now, God's Word is not a primary shaping factor for the next generation. A 2021 survey found that only 11 percent of Americans read the Bible daily, and 29 percent never read the Bible.[3] Sadly, it's been said that millennials are the most likely demographic never to read the Bible. Since 63 percent of American adults consider themselves to be Christians, it's easy to see

---

3. "Frequency of Reading the Bible among Adults in the United States from 2018 to 2021," Statista, accessed June 20, 2022, www.statista.com/statistics/299433/bible-readership-in-the-usa/#:~:text=Bible%20readership%20in%20the%20U.S.%202018%2D2021&text=A%20survey%20from%202021%20found,to%2029%20percent%20of%20respondents.

the disconnect.[4] How is the next generation supposed to learn who God is if they don't know His Word? Instead of our children being shaped by the Bible, other sources are instructing them. Here's a perfect example: the average American spends three hours a day watching TV, not counting media consumed on personal devices.[5]

If we want to reach the next generation, we must find ways to teach them the Scriptures and encourage them to look to it as a source of knowledge and help. If you have children at home, create natural opportunities to talk about God by having a regular family devotion time at breakfast, dinnertime, or before bed. Read and discuss a book of the Bible together, perhaps one chapter a day. Talk about what the passage says and how you can obey it and apply it to your own lives. Post Bible verses around the house to keep the Scripture always before you.

If you don't have children in the home, find some young people with whom you can engage in Bible study.

---

4. Danielle Haynes, "Pew Poll: Number of Americans Who Identify as Christian Further Declines," UPI, December 14, 2021, www.upi.com/Top_News/US/2021/12/14/Pew-poll -religion/4101639510653/.
5. "Average Daily Time Spent Watching TV in the United States from 2019 to 2023," Statista, accessed June 20, 2022, www.statista.com/statistics/186833/average-television-use-per -person-in-the-us-since-2002/.

You don't have to be a great theologian to dissect the living Word with another person. Open your home or meet at a coffee shop. My heart is always blessed when I walk into my favorite coffee place and see two believers sitting at a table with their Bibles open. Sharing God's Word with one another and with the next generation needs to be more than a Sunday morning thing.

Pray. The second way you can plant seeds of faith in the next generation is through your prayers. I have heard countless stories of a person coming to know Christ as the result of the prayers of a faithful parent or grandparent. My Grandmother Howze prayed for me, and I believe her prayers had a profound effect on my life. My great-grandfather regularly prayed for all his grandchildren and great-grandchildren, and his prayers also bore much fruit.

James tells us, "Therefore confess your sins to each other and pray for each other so that you may be healed. The prayer of a righteous person is powerful and effective" (5:16). I love that confession of sin is linked to powerful prayers. All of us enter this world with both generational blessings and generational curses from our families of origin. All of us sin. But that need not affect our prayer life. James tells us that when we confess our sin and pray for one another, our prayers are powerful and effective because we remain in righteous standing with God.

Many books have been written on how to pray for our children. But seeking God on behalf of the next generation need not be complicated. We can pray Scripture over them. We can pray for their future spouses and children. We can pray for God to uphold them in the immediate struggles they face, that they would see the Lord's hand in everything they walk through. We can pray simply that God would draw their hearts to Himself and that they would walk devotedly with Him.

Prayer is a gift. The Lord invites us to approach His throne of grace with confidence to receive His help. As we pray for our children, we place them into His capable hands, believing that He will respond to our prayers with help and healing. Prayer also requires discipline. Most of our lives move quickly. If we don't schedule time to pray, other things will crowd it out.

It may not surprise you that the average person spends three hours on his or her phone each day[6] (and for baby boomers and younger people that number jumps to over

---

6. Trevor Wheelwright, "2022 Cell Phone Usage Statistics: How Obsessed Are We?," Reviews.org, January 24, 2022, www.reviews.org/mobile/cell-phone-addiction/#:~:text=On%20average%2C%20Americans%20spend%202,on%20their%20phones%20in%202022.

five hours!).[7] While it's hard to find consistent statistics for how long the average Christian spends in prayer each day, I can guarantee it's not three hours. Imagine how our spiritual lives might soar if we spent three hours a day—or even one hour—approaching God's throne on behalf of the next generation.

Create an attractive atmosphere. I am a big advocate for the truth that walking with Jesus is not boring. Growing up, my parents did a great job of making family life fun. We went bowling and skating, played little league baseball and basketball, and played outdoor games in the neighborhood. My dad was often the ringleader for all this recreation. Our friends came to our house like bees to a hive, and we all knew they were coming to joke around with dad.

Second Corinthians 2:15 says, "For we are to God the pleasing aroma of Christ among those who are being saved and those who are perishing." Our Christian walk shouldn't resemble drudgery. It should be attractive and inviting to outsiders. People have asked if I felt restricted by my parents' strict rules, and my answer is not really.

---

7. Eileen Brown, "Americans Spend Far More Time on Their Smartphones Than They Think," ZDNet, April 28, 2019, www.zdnet.com/article/americans-spend-far-more-time-on -their-smartphones-than-they-think/.

That's because my life was full of fun and laughter and good food and joy.

MAXIMIZE MEALTIMES

Let's talk about food for a moment. Not only do I associate being in God's house with the smell of delicious food, I also have countless good memories of sitting around the Winans' dining room table. At Christmastime, we didn't receive gifts from our parents (because they never embraced that part of Christmas), but the holiday still brimmed over with joy and cheer. We had good food, laughter, great music, and each other's company as we celebrated our Savior's birth.

In their book *The Hour That Matters Most*, Les and Leslie Parrot cite studies that show that the more often families eat together, the less likely kids are to engage in risky behaviors such as smoking, drinking, drugs, and eating disorders. And yet, only 30 percent of families eat meals together on a regular basis.[8] We live in such a fast-

---

8. Jill Anderson, "Harvard EdCast: The Benefit of Family Mealtime," Harvard Graduate School of Education, April 1, 2020, www.gse.harvard.edu/news/20/04/harvard-edcast-benefit -family-mealtime#:~:text=Family%20therapist%20Anne %20Fishel%20says,being%20hugely%20beneficial%20for %20kids.

paced society that making this happen can seem nearly impossible. But I think it's worth considering ways we can use mealtimes to build faith.

In the Jewish tradition, mealtimes are meaningful. God commanded His people to celebrate multiple feasts throughout the year. One of the most well-known is Passover. This meal, which symbolizes the Israelites' journey out of slavery in Egypt and into the Promised Land, teaches children about God's faithfulness and His promise of a Messiah. Each detail reveals something about God's character and His plan.

If you're still not convinced of the role of food (and sharing a meal) in passing on faith, consider the many references to banquets and feasting in Scripture—Numbers 10:10; Psalm 36:8; Song of Songs 2:4; Luke 14:15; Luke 15:23; to list a few. Banquets are mentioned as a means of celebration, sustenance, comfort, and even protection. Psalm 23:5 tells us this about our Good Shepherd: "You prepare a table before me in the presence of my enemies."

Food is one aspect of creating an attractive environment for passing on faith. The comfort and joy of following Jesus is meant to be experiential. Psalm 34:8 says, "Taste and see that the LORD is good; blessed is the one who takes refuge in Him." I never had to guess what this verse was talking about. My walk with God literally involved tasting good things.

Be present. One thing my parents did well was to be present. When they weren't at work, mom and dad were available to us. We didn't have to work hard to have a conversation with our parents. They were simply *there*—physically and emotionally present.

I tried to emulate this quality when my kids were young. All the years I had a regular tour schedule, I made it a priority to fly home after many concerts so that I could spend time with my family. I wanted to be there in the morning to have breakfast with my kids and pray for them before they went to school. Sometimes these decisions came with a financial cost or the loss of certain opportunities, but I don't regret it. Being there had a profound impact on my marriage and our children.

Being present in the lives of young people is necessary for the conversations mentioned in Deuteronomy 6. These faith discussions are happening in mundane moments—sitting at home, walking along the road, going to bed, and getting up. We need to be present in those moments. Even if your children are older or out of the house, it's never too late to offer the gift of your presence. Thanks to technology, it's easy to schedule a phone call while you're driving or taking a walk.

Research shows that parents spend more time with their children than parents did fifty years ago. However, today's children must compete with cell phones for their parents' attention. Brandon McDaniel, a researcher on family relationships, has called this phenomenon "technoference," and experts are concerned of its long-term impact on children.[9] Our obsession with checking our phones not only impacts family relationships, it can also impede our ability to transfer our faith values to the next generation. Being physically and emotionally available to our children is critical to their spiritual development. We must create spaces for discussing God, His ways, and His plan in our everyday lives.

Support spiritual growth. As I have already mentioned, helping our young people find their place in the church is vital to passing on faith. If our top priority is for the next generation to know and follow Jesus, we must prioritize activities that lead to spiritual

9. Annabelle Timsit, "Smartphones Are Disrupting the Crucial Connections between Parents and Their Babies," Quartz, July 31, 2019, https://qz.com/1674835/technology-is-interfering -with-the-parent-child-relationship/.

knowledge and growth. Part of this is encouraging and enabling your children to regularly attend church and other groups and functions that build faith. My parents paid special attention to the activities in which we were involved. They made sure we got to youth group, Bible studies, and choir rehearsal.

Another way to support spiritual growth is to provide Christian resources. We can make sure our young people have a user-friendly Bible, devotionals, and books on theology and Christian living. If they don't like to read, connect them with audiobooks, podcasts, or online sermons they might enjoy. And don't underestimate the power of Christian music. My parents only allowed Christian music in the home. Not only did we gain an appreciation for artists such as Shirley Caesar, Andraé Crouch, and so many more, but the words of those gospel songs touched our hearts and grounded us in the truths of God's Word. I love playing worship music for my grandson, Wyatt, and seeing him worship the Lord in his sweet toddler way.

Another method of encouraging faith is to provide opportunities to serve. Most churches need volunteers in multiple areas. Church work days, community outreaches, and mission trips are ideal places for youth to serve.

PUTTING IT TOGETHER

When I think back to my childhood, my parents and their generation excelled at doing the work. They taught us the Word, encouraged Christian fellowship, and taught us to pray and fast. Each year at Christmastime (and sometimes on Mother's Day), the Winans family put on a concert for the community at Detroit's Mercy College. I'm not sure how my parents scraped together the funds to sponsor those Christmas concerts, but they did. They invited all of Detroit to join us for an evening centered on love and family. Mom and Dad wanted to remind everyone of the true reason we celebrate Christmas—Jesus, who came to be God with us and save the world.

Offering this gift of music to the community filled my soul with joy and brought home the true meaning of being blessed. Being blessed in the Lord isn't about material things; it's about His love flowing through you. To put on those concerts, we spent months planning, selecting music, arranging, rehearsing, and gathering the equipment we needed. We learned how to work together, sing together, and use our individual gifts. Looking back, putting on those concerts was one of the greatest gifts our parents could have given us.

Those events, which filled out the seven hundred seats of the auditorium, paved the way for us to become professional musicians and performers. Serving the community with my family was a blessing and reminded me that part of my purpose as a Christ-follower was to serve others and share the gospel. I realized I could overcome my shyness, contribute to the kingdom, and tell others about the hope I had.

The generation behind me—they did the work. My parents and grandparents studied the Word, they taught, they corrected, they upheld truth, they loved, they prayed, they served. They gave me the gift of their presence and taught me how to be a colaborer with Christ. I wouldn't be the woman I am without their tireless investment. They embodied Colossians 3:23–24, which says, "Whatever you do, work at it with all your heart, as working for the Lord, not for human masters, since you know that you will receive an inheritance from the Lord as a reward. It is the Lord Christ you are serving."

Passing on faith to the next generation requires work, but it's work worth doing, because the reward is great. And the best part is, we don't do the work alone.

- Who in your life has put in the work of training you spiritually? (It may be a parent, a pastor, or a mentor.) How has this person enhanced your walk of faith?

_____

_____

_____

- What are some ways you can lay the foundation of faith in your home, specifically in the next generation?

_____

_____

_____

- Which disciplines do you see as most overlooked and necessary?

_____

_____

_____

five

YOU NEED THE HOLY SPIRIT

I grew up in a church where the preaching was fiery and the Holy Ghost was real. My great-grandfather Winans told my father, David, incredible stories from his early ministry in the Church of God in Christ. He spoke about saints seeing prison doors swing open in the manner of the apostle Peter, and he told of people coming back from the dead. Our church, which had been founded by my great-grandfather, believed in salvation through faith and being filled with the Holy Spirit. The evidence of that filling came through speaking in tongues and prophecy, along with all the spiritual gifts. Growing up in a Pentecostal church, I never doubted the power or necessity of the Holy Spirit in the believer's life. The Spirit of God wasn't some impersonal force—He was a Person, a Helper. And we needed Him.

As I was growing up, I observed how my parents depended on the Holy Spirit in their everyday lives. If the work they were doing for the kingdom was an engine, the Holy Spirit was the gasoline. They recognized the need to rely on Him daily for the work God had called them to do, both as parents and as ministers of the gospel of Jesus Christ. Something else I picked up as a child is that the Holy Spirit is exciting! With Him, *anything* could happen. Prison doors could shake open, the blind could see again, the enslaved person could go free, and the sick could be made well. The best part was, as a believer, I had constant access to the Holy Spirit's power in my life.

As Jesus was sharing a final meal with His disciples in the upper room, He began telling them about the Helper He would send: "I will ask the Father, and he will give you another advocate to help you and be with you forever—the Spirit of truth. The world cannot accept him, because it neither sees him nor knows him. But you know him, for he lives with you and will be in you" (John 14:16–17). The Greek word translated "advocate" or "helper" in our English translations is *parakletos* and denotes legal counsel.

I occasionally indulge in watching a crime drama. In those shows, when a suspect receives a hard question, they'll often exclaim, "I want my lawyer!" The Holy Spirit is that kind of help when we're in trouble. He knows exactly what's going on and can give us wise counsel. Right off the bat, Jesus tells His disciples that this Helper will be rejected by the world. Only believers will be aware of His presence because He will be with them and in them.

In the same conversation, Jesus reveals another function of the Spirit: "But the Helper, the Holy Spirit, whom the Father will send in my name, he will teach you all things and bring to your remembrance all that I have said to you" (John 14:26, ESV). The Holy Spirit helps us understand Scripture, the gospel message, and Jesus's teachings. We cannot hope to pass on faith to the next generation without the Holy Spirit's help.

OH, THE THINGS THE SPIRIT CAN DO

In my experience, many Christians underestimate their need for the Holy Spirit's guidance and help in their daily lives. I remember a day several years ago when I was praying. All of a sudden I felt an urgency to pray in the Spirit. My heart was heavy, and I didn't know why. I continued to pray in the Spirit until the heaviness lifted. After I stopped praying, I looked to see what time it was. I later found out that at the exact moment I was praying in the Spirit, my sister Debbie had an accident that could have taken her sight. I realized the Holy Spirit had prompted me to intercede on her behalf. Thank you, Jesus, for the Holy Spirit!

Have you ever watched a marching band moving in perfect unison? Each musician moves in uniform step as the band executes precise movements and formations. It's amazing to watch. Galatians 5:25 says, "Since we live by the Spirit, let us keep in step with the Spirit." When Paul spoke these words to the church in Galatia, this was still a new way of relating to God. Before Jesus came, the Jews had followed the law—the Old Testament commands— so living by the Spirit instead of a list of rules was a novel concept—so much so that the Galatians were struggling with legalism and the temptation to depend on their own obedience to the law rather than Jesus's transformative work on the cross.

Paul describes "living by the Spirit" as staying in step with the Spirit as we walk out our faith. Like the march- ing band, the believer is to mimic the Spirit's movements and follow His promptings. In this way, all believers everywhere can move in unison to carry out God's plan.

Let's look at just a few ways the Holy Spirit helps us in our mission of passing on faith.

The Holy Spirit empowers believers to share the gospel. In Acts 1:8, Jesus commissioned His disciples with these words: "But you will receive power when the Holy Spirit comes on you; and you will be my witnesses in Jerusalem, and in all Judea and Samaria, and to the ends of the earth." The Holy Spirit provides the power for us to spread the gospel to others. We cannot hope to see transformation in the next generation if we are not relying on the power of God for their salvation and spiritual growth.

Something I learned long ago is that I cannot save anyone; the Holy Spirit must do that work. But I can be a witness. I can tell others about what God has done in my life. As the Holy Spirit empowers me to boldly share the Good News with others, I can trust Him for the result.

The Holy Spirit provides wisdom and knowledge. Scripture tells us that the Spirit bestows special revelation on believers. In Ephesians 1:17–20, the apostle Paul fleshes out this concept:

> I keep asking that the God of our Lord Jesus Christ, the glorious Father, may give you the Spirit of wisdom and revelation, so that you may know him better. I pray that the eyes of your

heart may be enlightened in order that you may know the hope to which he has called you, the riches of his glorious inheritance in his holy people, and his incomparably great power for us who believe. That power is the same as the mighty strength he exerted when he raised Christ from the dead and seated him at his right hand in the heavenly realms.

The Holy Spirit allows us to know God better by opening the eyes of our hearts. Before salvation, our hearts are blind to the things of God. But the Holy Spirit gives us our spiritual sight, allowing us to be filled with His hope and view the riches and power we have in Him. This is sometimes a very different reality than what we see in the world around us. Realizing we have access to the same power that raised Jesus from the dead is a game changer. The success of our mission is not contingent on our own strength or resources—far from it. As we allow the Holy Spirit to reveal the things of God to us, we can more easily join Him in what He is doing in the lives of those around us.

The Holy Spirit guides the believer into truth. We have already established that the spirit of the age is one of chaos and deceit. We live in a world that encourages us to embrace and speak our own truth. It tries to convince us that there are many truths and many ways to God. But among those many competing voices, Jesus says, "I am the way and the truth and the life. No one comes to the Father except through me" (John 14:6). This declaration can sound harsh to our modern ears. How could there be only one way to God? But this is our Savior's claim, and part of the role of the Holy Spirit is to guide us into absolute truth.

Jesus told His disciples, "But when he, the Spirit of truth, comes, he will guide you into all the truth. He will not speak on his own; he will speak only what he hears, and he will tell you what is yet to come" (John 16:13).

The next generation is in desperate need of God's truth. Our world is in a state of confusion, where many voices claim to be the truth and it can be difficult to spot the deception. I like to picture an airplane being guided down onto a runway by air traffic control. Like the voice in the pilot's headset, the Holy Spirit gently guides us to a perfect landing onto the runway of God's truth. That's why 1 John 4:1 tells us to "test the spirits" to discern which promptings are from the Lord. The lies shouted by the culture may surround us, but we can depend on the Holy Spirit to direct us to God's truth so we can guide others to that same truth.

The Holy Spirit intercedes for us and helps us in our weaknesses. Nothing showed me my weakness more than being a parent. From the moment my son, Alvin III, was placed in my arms, I felt the full weight of my inadequacy to raise this little human, both physically and spiritually. As that baby grew into a precious little boy, a spirited teenager, and an intelligent and strong-willed young man, I needed even more of the Spirit's help to rise above my shortcomings as a mother and guide him to the truth. And then came Ashley, a completely different little human, with a different personality and set of needs. And she tested me much more than my son, bless her little heart, so the Spirit had to give me wisdom to guide her down the path He had for her.

Throughout my life I have faced moments when I didn't know what to do or the right decision to make. Scripture tells us that in those moments, the Holy Spirit pleads with the Father on our behalf, helping us fall into line with God's will.

Romans 8:26–27 offers these words of comfort: "In the same way, the Spirit helps us in our weakness. We do not know what we ought to pray for, but the Spirit himself intercedes for us through wordless groans. And he who searches our hearts knows the mind of the Spirit, because the Spirit intercedes for God's people in accordance with the will of God."

In our mission to pass on faith to the next generation, we will face moments when we have no idea what to do. When my son moved to Australia to get space from us and do his own thing, my husband and I had to let him go and entrust his path to the Lord. But as I prayed for God's will to be done in Alvin's life, the Holy Spirit, knowing all the hearts involved, and the mind of God, joined me in my pleas. What an extraordinary gift God offers us through His Holy Spirit.

The Holy Spirit does the work of salvation. While God calls us to be diligent in teaching the next generation about who He is and what He has done, the Holy Spirit is the true Hero here. The Spirit works in people's lives to draw them, save them, and transform their lives. We can do none of those things. Romans 8:11 tells us, "If the Spirit of him who raised Jesus from the dead is living in you, he who raised Christ from the dead will also give life to your mortal bodies because of his Spirit who lives in you."

Realizing that the Holy Spirit does the work takes the pressure off. We can work as unto the Lord in freedom and joy, knowing that He is the One Who does the work. This is good news because He can do so much more than we ever could. Paul lends some perspective when he addresses the believers in Corinth, who had been engaging in squabbles over which teacher was greater—Paul or Apollos. Paul chides them in 1 Corinthians 3:5–9, saying,

> What, after all, is Apollos? And what is Paul? Only servants, through whom you came to believe—as the Lord has assigned to each his task. I planted the seed, Apollos watered it, but God has been making it grow. So neither the one who plants nor the one who waters is anything, but only God, who makes things grow. The one who plants and the one who waters have one purpose, and they will each be rewarded according to their own labor. For we are co-workers in God's service; you are God's field, God's building.

I love how this passage illuminates both sides of the equation. The work matters. As coworkers in God's service, we are accountable for the planting we do or do not do. But at the end of the day, God does the work. He makes things grow. We can leave the results in His capable hands and trust the Holy Spirit to do His thing.

Salvation is just the beginning of the Holy Spirit's work in the life of a believer. Sanctification is an ongoing process of turning from the sinful acts of the flesh (Galatians 5:16–21) and keeping in step with the Spirit in order to bear good fruit (Galatians 5:22–25). The Holy Spirit also distributes spiritual gifts to believers (1 Corinthians 12:7–11), is a seal for their salvation (Ephesians 1:13), and convicts the world of sin (John 16:8).

A NEW WAY TO LIVE

The day of Pentecost described in Acts 2 must have been a sight to behold. Scripture says that as Peter and the other apostles were together, a sound like that of a violent wind filled the whole house where they were sitting: "They saw what seemed to be tongues of fire that separated and came to rest on each of them. All of them were filled with the Holy Spirit and began to speak in other tongues as the Spirit enabled them" (3–4). Hearing the sound, a group of God-fearing Jews from every nation who were staying in Jerusalem gathered to find out what was going on. They were shocked to discover they could hear the apostles speaking in their own languages. Peter preached the gospel, and three thousand people believed and were baptized.

This dramatic scene happened about ten days after Jesus had left the earth. During the forty days following His resurrection, Jesus appeared to His disciples and more than five hundred people, giving them "many convincing proofs" he was alive, and preaching to them about the kingdom of God (1 Corinthians 15:6). Jesus instructed them not to leave Jerusalem until they received the baptism of the Holy Spirit (Acts 1:4–5). Before he ascended into heaven, He charged them to be His witnesses to the ends of the earth. Ten days later, the Spirit showed up. *Whew!* Does the Holy Spirit know how to make an entrance or what? Although the Spirit is always working behind the scenes, He can be flashy when the situation warrants.

The Holy Spirit didn't quietly sneak in while the apostles were asleep. There could be no doubt that this was *it*, that this was the advocate Jesus had promised. I love the diversity described in these passages. God-fearing Jews from every nation were present—Africans, Asians, and Middle Easterners, along with others. Many who received the Spirit that day would return to their own parts of the world, setting in motion Jesus's commission to take the gospel to the ends of the earth.

Another thing I love about this narrative is that Peter quotes the prophet Joel speaking about the generations:

In the last days, God says,
I will pour out my Spirit on all people.
Your sons and daughters will prophesy,

your young men will see visions,
your old men will dream dreams.
Even on my servants, both men and women,
I will pour out my Spirit in those days,
and they will prophesy. (Acts 2:17–18)

This speaks loudly to the fact that the Holy Spirit is for all believers, both young and old. There is no junior Holy Spirit. Through His Spirit, God will use all generations to reveal Himself to the world. I hope you are starting to grasp the great gift the Holy Spirit is to us in our quest to pass on faith. We simply cannot do it without Him. Here are three ways the Holy Spirit helps us pass on faith to the next generation.

The Holy Spirit gives us revelation and discernment to work with individuals. One of my biggest regrets as a parent is that I sometimes employed a one-size-fits-all method of raising my children. My parents' way of doing things had worked for me and my siblings, so I just tried to replicate what they had done. However, my son and daughter were two very different people with different personalities, needs, and motivators. I wish I had invited the Holy Spirit more into the process of raising my children and relied on Him more to give me wisdom for parenting each individual child.

In some ways, my grandson, Wyatt, is a sweet do-over. As I teach him about God, I seek the Holy Spirit for what my grandson's spirit needs. When he is upset, instead of looking for behavior modification, I seek to bring the peace of God into the situation. As I invite the Holy Spirit into our interactions, He gives me insight to lead my grandson in a godly direction.

When you look at the day of Pentecost, the Spirit provided for each person to hear the message in his or her own language, providing them a personal encounter with the Savior. The Spirit can help us assess our audience—whether a child, a grandchild, or a young person we mentor—and give us specific wisdom and insight on how to share His truth with that person.

The Holy Spirit creates opportunities. Part of passing on our faith to our children is being aware of teachable moments or opportunities to engage with spiritual truth. Sometimes these openings occur in mundane settings such as sitting at the breakfast table or riding in the car. Other times, the Spirit may provide something more unusual to set the stage for an important spiritual conversation. When my children were teens, there were many times the Holy Spirit would prompt me to sit down and ask one of them a series of questions to make sure they were doing well beneath the surface. Sometimes I felt the urge to go to their bedroom and check a few drawers. In those moments, I discovered things I needed to address that I would not have known had I not followed the Holy Spirit's lead.

I love the story of Philip and the Ethiopian recorded in Acts 8. The apostles had gone out to different regions to preach the good news, cast out evil spirits, and heal people. One day an angel of the Lord comes to Philip and tells him to walk down a specific road.

Have you ever experienced these kinds of detailed instructions? An inner voice that tells you to go talk to a particular person or go back inside a building? I'm reminded of a story my grandmother shared with me many years ago. One night as she was walking home, the Holy Spirit prompted her to go a different way than her usual route. She later found out there had been a man with a knife walking on the path she would normally take. The Holy Spirit used her obedience to possibly spare her life.

In this case, Philip starts down the road and soon comes upon an Ethiopian eunuch, who happens to be a treasurer for the Queen of Ethiopia. The man had recently been in Jerusalem to worship, and he was on his way home. As he travels, he is reading the book of Isaiah, the prophet, when lo and behold, Philip just happens to come along. Then, "the Spirit told Philip, 'Go to that chariot and stay near it'" (8:29). When Philip gets close to the chariot, he overhears the man reading Isaiah and asks if he understands what he's reading. The Ethiopian admits he doesn't and invites Philip into his chariot to explain the passage to him.

This is my favorite part: Philip uses the passage the man is reading to tell him the good news about Jesus! Next, they drive by some water and the man asks to be baptized. Philip gladly obliges. And lest we forget the Holy Spirit made this whole thing happen, verse 39 reminds us: "When they came up out of the water, the Spirit of the Lord suddenly took Philip away, and the eunuch did not see him again, but went on his way rejoicing."

That's what I like to call a divine appointment. It ended with rejoicing and pizzazz! More than that, it ended with someone being drawn into the kingdom of God. The Holy Spirit specializes in such non-random appointments. As we ask the Helper to give us opportunities, our eyes will be opened to the assignments He is providing every day. I like to start the day by asking, "Lord, what divine appointments do you have for me today? Help me keep in step with You."

The Holy Spirit empowers us and gives us words to speak. Have you ever watched a group of improvisational actors perform? They are incredible. They can take a suggestion from the audience and come up with a complex scene on the spot. I love to improvise with my singing, but I'm baffled by those who can act out entire scenes without preparation. The Bible tells us that the Holy Spirit empowers us to be spiritually quick on our feet.

Jesus even advocated for spiritual improv when he gave these instructions in Luke 12:11–12: "When you are brought before synagogues, rulers and authorities, do not worry about how you will defend yourselves or what you will say, for the Holy Spirit will teach you at that time what you should say." Even in the most challenging or tense conversations, the Holy Spirit gives us the words to say. When I think back on some of the more difficult discussions I've had with my children, I can see how when my heart was right, the Spirit gave me exactly the right words to say. In fact, sometimes I'm surprised at what He said through me. Thanks to the Holy Spirit, we don't have to be great theologians or orators to effectively guide our children through the truths of God's Word.

Growing up Pentecostal taught me at a young age the power of the Holy Spirit. I saw it when I sang that first solo and eyes in the audience filled with tears. I saw it in how He guided me through my career, continually

We plant the seeds,
but God makes them grow.

leading me to opportunities to use my gifts and proclaim His name. I saw it when my children submitted their lives to Christ, and He changed their hearts in ways I could never have imagined, even as their mother. I saw it when I felt supernatural comfort in my darkest moments. And I saw it when He called my husband, Alvin, and I to start a church and He blessed that body beyond what we could have dreamed.

The work is important, yes, but we must understand the necessity of the Holy Spirit. He's not optional—not if we want to have peace and hope and power in our lives. The devil comes to steal, kill, and destroy, and he comes every day. He never stops showing up. But neither does the Holy Spirit. He is always there, providing power and help to the believer. We plant the seeds, but God makes them grow.

QUESTIONS *to* CONSIDER

- Which aspect of the Holy Spirit is most meaningful to you? Examples are help, presence, guidance, intercession, empowerment, and so on.

  _____

  _____

  _____

- Talk about a time when you felt the Holy Spirit's prompting. What happened?

  _____

  _____

  _____

- How does our call to "work as unto the Lord" coincide with our dependence on the Holy Spirit?

  _____

  _____

  _____

CHAPTER

six

POURING FROM A FULL CUP

When I was growing up, I was taught two ways to address any problem in life: the Word and prayer. My parents instilled in me that the Bible contained the answer to every problem, and the prayer of the righteous could be wielded to bring about help and deliverance in any situation. They weren't wrong. God's Word *does* contain insight for every circumstance, and it *does* lead to blessings in the believer's life. In fact, Joshua 1:8 promises that as we meditate on the Word and do what it says, we will be "prosperous and successful."

Growing up, the two-step program of reading the Bible and prayer made sense to me. More than that, it worked! Not only did I watch my parents draw their strength from these basic Christian disciplines, but by God's grace, within the support of my Christ-centered family, I grew into a strong, whole person. What my parents and those in their generation gave me was the ability to live life from a place of being whole. I'm thankful they pointed us to Scripture because that foundation has fortified me and pulled me through many difficult times; I understand not everyone has that. While I took it for granted, I have come to realize my trauma-free, Christian upbringing is not the norm.

When Alvin and I started Nashville Life Church, we encountered brokenness on many different levels. A good number of the people, young and old, who flooded into the church had experienced trauma or abuse. Some of them had never seen an example of a healthy relationship, let alone a loving marriage. We quickly realized we were dealing with some heavy issues within our congregation, including trauma, anxiety, depression, addiction, and other mental and emotional health struggles. Still, we believed that God's desire for each person was wholeness and healing.

God is into wholeness. We have already discussed the aspects of passing on the faith in Deuteronomy 6, but look at verses 4 and 5: "Hear, O Israel: The LORD our God, the LORD is one. Love the LORD your God with all your heart and with all your soul and with all your strength." This passage is called the *shema* (pronounced "shuh-MAH"), a Hebrew word that means listen, hear, or take heed. Moses delivered the *shema*, which became a daily prayer for the Israelites, just before he told them to pass God's commands down to their children. This was to be their heart posture as they taught the next generation about Him.

The passage begins by saying, "The Lord our God, the Lord is one." God is whole. He is One. He sets the perfect standard for wholeness, and our wholeness is found through Him. Next, the Scripture commands the people to love God with all their "heart, soul, and strength." (Jesus famously repeated the *shema* in Mark 12:29–31, adding that the second commandment was to love our neighbor as ourselves.) When we're healthy and whole—body, soul, and mind—we are able to love God and others with all we are. If I want to love God with all my heart, there is no room for unforgiveness, bitterness, or self-loathing. If I desire to love Him with all my soul, I must allow for my soul to be cared for. And loving God with my strength isn't only about physical strength; my mental and emotional strength also matter. To love God fully and pass that on to others, I must constantly invite Him to heal and renew my heart, soul, and mind.

To love God fully and
pass that on to others,
I must constantly invite
Him to heal and renew my
heart, soul, and mind.

———————

This isn't an easy task, because we have an enemy. In John 10:10 Jesus says, "The thief comes only to steal and kill and destroy; I came that they may have life and have it abundantly" (ESV). The enemy has a strategy to take down our souls and keep us from the tasks God has for us to do. But Jesus offers us abundant life. The Greek word for abundant is *perissos*, and among its meanings are "above and beyond," "superabundant," "superior," and "excessive." Jesus offers us a better way to live—a way we can experience His goodness and be grateful for the blessings in our lives. And His way of living is over the top, far superior to other ways of living. He cares about our physical, emotional, psychological, social, and spiritual well-being. He created us and knows how these things are all connected.

If the life Jesus offers is above and beyond, superabundant, excessively good, why do we see such a different picture of our world? Are we failing to unlock and take hold of the grace-filled life Jesus offers? I think that's a part of it. Is the enemy winning more than he should on the battleground of our mental and emotional health? Absolutely. But another important factor to consider is the simple reality that our natural world is corrupted by the effects of sin and the fall. And as a result, we've got problems.

Paul described it this way: "We know that the whole creation has been groaning as in the pains of childbirth right up to the present time" (Romans 8:22). We live in fallen bodies with fallen brains and fallen chemical reactions. This is all part of the groaning Paul describes. Every generation has its problems. Unfortunately, statistics reveal that the mental health crisis in our world is growing.

During the past few years, as the COVID-19 pandemic changed our lives in significant ways, reported instances of anxiety, depression, stress, and other disorders in both adults and children rose significantly.[1] The number of those saying they experienced suicidal thoughts also increased sharply. And while social media connects us in ways we could only dream of in the past, its primary users—millennials—are the loneliest generation. According to data, 30 percent of millennials say they

---

1. Kayla N. Anderson, Lakshmi Radhakrishnan, Rashon I. Lane, et al., "Changes and Inequities in Adult Mental Health-Related Emergency Department Visits during the COVID-19 Pandemic in the US," *Jama Psychiatry* 79, no. 5 (2022): 475–485, https://doi.org/10.1001/jamapsychiatry.2022.0164; "The State of Mental Health in America," Mental Health America, accessed June 20, 2022, www.mhanational.org/issues/state-mental-health-america.

"always or often" feel lonely, and 22 percent say they have no friends.[2]

These statistics are important for us to consider, because when our own mental health is in disarray, we can't effectively love our neighbor and pass on faith to others. You can't pour out of an empty cup. When I interviewed Tabitha Brown, influencer, actress, and author of *Feeding the Soul*, for Generations Live, she described her healing journey, which was both physical and emotional. Earlier in her life, she explained, she had put everyone else's needs above her own, something many women can relate to. She poured into her husband and children and friends until she was depleted physically, emotionally, and even spiritually.

"I love my family," she said in her effervescent manner, "but, honey, without me being full Tab, I had nothing to give. I had to do that self-work and tell myself some hard truths. We'll lie to ourselves and tell ourselves we're alright. I had to tell Tab the truth."

---

2. Jamie Ballard, "Millennials Are the Loneliest Generation," YouGov, July 30, 2019, https://today.yougov.com/topics/lifestyle/articles-reports/2019/07/30/loneliness-friendship-new-friends-poll-survey.

She described talking to herself in the mirror one day, trying to give herself some encouragement. As she spoke, she realized she was whispering, even though she was the only one at home. "I realized I was afraid of me, because I didn't know who I was," she said. That moment was profound, because she realized she'd been playing a part to make others happy and it was taking a toll on her mental health.

"Make sure you know who you are," she exhorted the women at the conference. "If we don't know who we are, we'll take anything, we won't stand for anything, we'll let people treat us any kind of way, and we won't treat ourselves well. We deserve to be well."

I agree that wellness is God's desire and design for you and me. From a place of wellness, I can better fulfill His purposes in my life. However, for that to happen, I must acknowledge the truth of who I am—who God created me to be—and allow His Holy Spirit to fill me. That may involve allowing Him to do some repairs on my cup. I love the encouragement contained in Romans 15:13: "May the God of hope fill you with all joy and peace as you trust in him, so that you may overflow with hope by the power of the Holy Spirit." As we trust in God, He fills us to overflowing with joy, peace, and hope through the power of the Holy Spirit.

BONE DRY

When I was the young mom of two toddlers and had a busy recording and touring schedule, I felt depleted on many days. I felt so many people needed things from me, and I was stretched so thin. I know this is a common feeling among mothers. My daughter, Ashley, is a mother herself now, and it's amazing to be reminded of how much time, energy, and attention those sweet little babies require.

When I was in that season, I often felt like my own wants and needs were selfish. When that check engine light of my soul would come on because I was exhausted, irritable, or dropping the ball, I'd ignore it and keep driving. Meanwhile, I felt guilty, as though I was letting everyone down. That mindset pushed me further away from Jesus's abundant, grace-filled, overflowing-with-hope life. I *knew* that His desire for me was wholeness of my body, mind, and spirit, but I didn't always do what was necessary to protect my emotional health.

As I look around, I think our culture perpetuates mental health struggles. Smartphones, social media, workaholism, and the rushed pace of life all contribute to the mental health crisis we're seeing around us, even among our young people. I am so thankful social media wasn't a thing when I was raising my children. Mom guilt was bad enough without scrolling through a feed and seeing the photo evidence of other moms doing it better. The comparison, worry, and discouragement social media can induce is so far from the abundant life Jesus died to give us.

One day everyone who believes in Jesus is going to heaven, where heartache and pain will cease to exist. But I want you to hear this: God means us to experience His abundant, Spirit-filled life down here right now! We must do what is necessary to allow the Holy Spirit to fill our cup so that we can effectively pour into others. Let's consider a few ways we can do this.

Be alert to the problem. We must acknowledge that mental health challenges, including mental illness, are a significant problem in our world. Mental illness is connected to other destructive issues, such as crime, homelessness, addiction, mass shootings, and suicide. As we look for ways to address these problems, we must also keep in mind whose influence is responsible for such devastation. We've already looked at 1 Peter 5:8 once, but let's consider its warning again: "Be alert and of sober mind. Your enemy the devil prowls around like a roaring lion looking for someone to devour."

At the time when Peter was preaching, Emperor Nero persecuted the Christians by throwing them into arenas to watch them be mauled and killed by wild animals. I wonder if the apostle had this mental picture in mind when he described our enemy. Satan is aggressive and proactive in his goal of killing our souls and keeping us from telling others about the hope found in Jesus. While God is far more powerful, we shouldn't underestimate Satan's ability to wreak havoc on our lives and emotional health. We must be alert to his schemes so that we can resist them.

Pay attention to your check engine light. We all know those moments when we feel at a breaking point. Maybe you have a stressful job, and you're burning the candle at both ends. Perhaps you're a mom of young children, and the demands of life are flying at you at a dizzying pace. Maybe you're carrying unresolved trauma, or you've been in a season when you've taken an emotional beating. Perhaps you've just been feeling low-grade sadness for months with no change, and you wonder if you'll ever feel like yourself again.

These are the moments to sit up and pay attention. Has the check engine light of your soul turned on? These vulnerable moments can create opportunities for the enemy to swoop in and attempt to "steal, kill, and destroy" what God is doing in your life. When warning signs pop up, don't wait to take a deeper look. Be proactive. Don't allow the seed of unhealth to take root. Talk to someone about what you're feeling and experiencing.

Develop a strategy. If wholeness is our goal, we must proactively address emotional health struggles the same way we tackle other problems in our lives. As always, we start with the Word of God and prayer. *We must be in the Word.* At the Generations Live conference, Dr. Charlotte Gambill talked about letting God do surgery on our spiritual eyes before we lose our vision. The Bible tells us in Hebrews 4:12, "The word of God is alive and active. Sharper than any double-edged sword, it penetrates even to dividing soul and spirit, joints and marrow; it judges the thoughts and attitudes of the heart." The living Word of God does surgery on our souls. As we pursue wholeness, we must be in His healing Word every day.

Prayer is another powerful tool in our quest for emotional health. Psalm 30:2 tells us, "LORD my God, I called to you for help, and you healed me." Healing comes through prayer and the Word of God. So many times I have fought through difficult circumstances on my knees. I saw my grandmother, father, and mother do this. I know the power of prayer. I have also asked my brothers and sisters in Christ to pray with me. We need intercessors— people to pray with and for us—in our lives, especially in times of struggle or suffering.

While the Word and prayer should be our primary means of soul care, sometimes the battle may be bigger and require a more robust game plan. When I had Dr. Anita Phillips on the *Generations* show, she shared some powerful truths about how mental illness interacts with our spiritual lives. Dr. Phillips, who is a trauma therapist, life coach, and host of the *In the Light* podcast, has extensive experience with the topic of mental health, including having a sister who struggled with mental illness. She pointed out that just like physical health, mental health is a continuum. Each of us falls somewhere on a scale between optimal emotional health and severe mental illness. This should cause us to pay attention to our mental health, even if our symptoms aren't as severe as someone else's. We should all check in with ourselves to see where we are on the continuum and if we need support.

Ephesians 6:12 tells us that our battle is not primarily physical. Forces in the spiritual realm battle for our souls, and the enemy, who is crafty, will use our thoughts and emotions to gain a foothold. Ephesians 6 tells us to put on our gear—the full armor of God—which includes the belt of truth, the breastplate of righteousness, sandals of the readiness of the gospel of peace, the shield of faith, the helmet of salvation, and the sword of the spirit, which is the Word of God. We're encouraged to "pray in the Spirit on all occasions" as we engage in this warfare (Ephesians 6:18). So many of our battles contain this spiritual element, and God does not leave us unprepared or ill-equipped.

In every battle, you must also have a strategy. As we understand more about how emotions work and the landscape of the battlefield in our minds, we can lean into these strategies, which include finding community that can help us stand strong, engaging in habits of self-care, seeking out professional counseling, and pursuing medical attention when we find ourselves in a crisis.

"We have learned how the engine works," Dr. Phillips said about the training professional therapists receive. "God's creativity is infinite, but the problems our minds and bodies encounter are repetitive. When your car isn't working right, you take it to the mechanic. When you have cancer, you go to the doctor and begin a treatment plan. When your mental health is going down, you should go see a counselor. Prayer and the Word are weapons; therapy is a strategy."

Your strategy for increasing your mental health may include therapy. Maybe it includes taking better care of your body through nutrition and exercise to balance hormones. Perhaps you need to go to bed earlier and wake up earlier so you can start your day in the Word and in prayer. Maybe you need to shut off your social media accounts. You may need to say no to things and decrease your commitments. You may need to make time in your week to meet with a friend for a heart-to-heart conversation and prayer or go on a date with your spouse. Each person's strategy for maintaining optimal emotional health will look different. Just make sure you have one.

Make space for emotional healing. When we are in a distressing place emotionally, we may be tempted to apply a quick fix and keep going. We must address emotional brokenness. Proverbs 15:13 says, "A happy heart makes the face cheerful, but heartache crushes the spirit." When our spirit has been crushed, we are spiritually vulnerable. But as we address our emotional health and bring it before the Lord and into the light of community, we allow God to fill us with His spiritual power.

Our emotions are not sin; the way we *handle* our emotions can be sin. Jesus felt every emotion but did not sin.

He is our sympathetic Savior, and there is no condem-
nation in Him. God doesn't remove the struggles of our
flesh when we trust in Him, and those struggles include
our thoughts and emotions.

One reason many of us don't experience emotional
healing is because we're ashamed to talk about what we're
going through. So many of us walk through suffering and
pain in isolation. This can create the illusion that we are
alone or the only one having this struggle.

At a recent women's event, surveys were passed out that
contained common struggles women face: low self-esteem,
feeling overwhelmed, infertility, body dysmorphia, sexual
shame, loneliness, and many more. Women were asked to
check the box on all struggles they were currently experiencing or had experienced in the past. After they had done
this (without writing their names on their papers), ushers
collected the surveys and redistributed them at random.

As the speaker read each struggle from stage—"loss of
a child," "eating disorder," "depression," "anxiety"—each
woman stood if the box was checked on the anonymous
survey she had received, symbolizing an actual woman
in the room. For many of the struggles listed, more than
half of the women stood. And when the speaker read
"loneliness," nearly every woman rose to her feet. After
the exercise, the women reported feeling relieved to know

they were not alone in these issues and emotions that plagued them. Knowing that others struggled with the same things offered hope and encouragement.

We need to be able to tell someone we trust that we are in the thick of battle or have been wounded by a past experience. Talking about our struggles, confessing sin, and applying God's truth from His Word frees us from shame and false guilt. Like a salve, the Word begins to heal our emotional wounds, but sometimes we need another to apply it. Looking back on moments when I struggled as a mom, in my marriage, and even now as a woman in my fifties, community and friendship made the difference between having a hard day and having a hard season. God has consistently used the people He's brought into my life to remind me of His love and that I can overcome through Him.

PASSING IT ON

As we acknowledge our need for emotional health and healing, and develop a strategy to address problem areas, God will meet us there. The power of the Holy Spirit makes us whole. And as we come to a place of greater wholeness and peace, we can invest what God has given us into the next generation.

Our kids need to understand how to be emotionally well in a world that regularly shows them the opposite. Some of the most popular shows for young people portray and normalize depravity, addiction, and emotional instability. We must ask the Holy Spirit to give us wisdom to minister to this generation and point them to the truth of God's unfailing, life-giving Word. What worked for our parents and grandparents won't necessarily work for the younger generations. When I was growing up, I could receive a harsh rebuke from my parents and hear it in love. But someone who grew up in an abusive home could hear the same exact words and receive them as abuse. It's a translation problem. I think this was the heart of Paul's words in 1 Corinthians 9:22: "To the weak I became weak, to win the weak. I have become all things to all people so that by all possible means I might save some."

It's OK and even imperative for those of us who are older and more experienced to take note of the specific emotional struggles of younger generations and cater to them in order that we might draw them into saving faith in Jesus Christ. As a mentor to the younger generation, I have had to learn how to express myself in different ways so that I don't offend or cause more damage to those I minister to. While the Word and prayer may have been sufficient for me to maintain my emotional health, someone else may require the help of a counselor or therapist to address his or her specific challenges. We are all at different places in our journey to emotional health, and we will only be made completely whole when Jesus returns and we spend eternity in His presence.

In the meantime, as we receive God's grace we can ask for wisdom to leave a legacy of emotional wellness and help the next generation chart a course to living the excessively good, abundant life Jesus offers. Our children need to know that our God can redeem their greatest heartaches and restore their crushed spirits. He is with them in suffering, and His love is better than life. Emotional wholeness is possible through Him.

- What is an action you need to take in pursuit of greater wholeness, mental health, and emotional wellness?

  _____

  _____

  _____

- What are some emotional struggles or barriers to wholeness that you have observed in your generation? In the next generation?

  _____

  _____

  _____

- What are some ways you can pour into the next generation in the area of emotional wellness?

  _____

  _____

  _____

CHAPTER

• seven •

IT'S ALL ABOUT RELATIONSHIP

Growing up with nine siblings, I was never lonely. There was always someone around to play with, joke with, get into trouble with, or sing with. There was no being an introvert in the Winans family—Lord knows, I tried. We were all up in each other's business. Being the firstborn girl with seven older brothers had its perks: I was little princess CeCe. It also had its liabilities: I sometimes got in trouble for joining in on my brothers' rowdy games. But I always knew I was loved by everyone in my family.

Some of my earliest memories are of my big brother, Ronald, taking time to play dolls with me. My younger sisters were still too little to play, so Ronald, a tall, dark, and handsome teenage boy, would help me do my doll's hair. He also taught me how to change the color of their hair with shoe polish. Though I shared a special relationship with each of my siblings, Ronald was my big teddy bear, protector, and nurturer. We shared a special bond.

Going to North Carolina with BeBe to sing with the PTL singers on the TV show *The PTL Club* was another special sibling experience. Although close in age, BeBe and I are two very different people. He was impulsive, passionate, and gregarious. I was quieter, reserved, and a verified homebody. But despite our differences, we had each other's backs. Over the years, we have gone on to produce seven albums together, attaining three Grammy Awards and numerous Dove Awards. I love the special singing relationship BeBe and I share.

From my earliest days, my family provided me with a sense of security and belonging, a feeling I can only describe as *home*. In my family, I was somebody. I was known and accepted for who I was. As siblings, we teased and poked fun at each other, but we were also each other's cheerleaders and friends. My siblings' love and acceptance were a representation to me of God's unconditional love. With Him, I am always at home.

Psalm 139:13–14 gives this powerful reminder: "For you created my inmost being; you knit me together in my mother's womb. I praise you because I am fearfully and wonderfully made; your works are wonderful, I know that full well." I'm grateful that my mom and dad and all my brothers and sisters helped me understand this truth. Each of them played a role in helping me discover the purpose and direction God had for me. Our shared history provided a powerful foundation of faith, which is one of the God-ordained functions of a family.

Research reveals that family relationships, especially between parents and children, play a vital role in the transmission of values, morals, and faith from one generation to the next. In *Passing on Faith*, Olwyn Mark writes,

> The passing on of faith invariably happens in every home. This involves the transmission— both actively and passively of values, attitudes, beliefs, and practices. These can be associated with a particular religious tradition or independent of any one institutional system of belief. No child enters adolescence and adulthood unaffected by the overarching story that they learn in the home.[1]

---

1. Olwyn Mark, *Passing on Faith* (London: Theos, 2016), 11.

That can be sobering to hear, can't it? Whether we realize it or not, who we are and how we live within the walls of our home deeply affect those who live with us. If my children always see me looking at my phone but they never observe me reading the Bible, they are receiving a story about my priorities. Enduring faith into adulthood is deeply influenced by the quality of relationships within the home.[2] Parents centered on Jesus naturally pass on faith to their children through a relationship with their children. Mark continues:

> Research reveals that high quality relationships in the home are key to successful faith transmission: Adolescents and young adults who experience or who have experienced close, affirming, and accepting relationships with both parents are more likely to identify with the beliefs and practices of their parents. The security and stability of the parent-child relationship, including the strength of the childhood attachment, informs the stability of future religious beliefs.[3]

2. Mark, *Passing on Faith*, 12.
3. Mark, *Passing on Faith*, 12.

I watched this play out in my family. My parents believed in discipline and training, but they were also nurturing. Dad would discipline you one moment and ask if you wanted some chips the next. Mom would unleash a righteous rebuke in love with a smile, never holding a grudge and always offering comfort. My parents consistently lived out what they were teaching us. When they made mistakes, they asked for forgiveness.

I understand that my experience can sound idealistic or not feasible in this century. But I share it because it worked. Modern parents may need to handle the details differently, but the basic principles are the same. Good family relationships don't happen by accident; they must be cultivated.

Maybe you didn't have the experience of growing up in a Christian home or you have not been living out faith in front of your children. Let me encourage you that you can absolutely start right now. Paul encourages us in Philippians 3:13–14, when he says, "One thing I do: Forgetting what is behind and straining toward what is ahead, I press on toward the goal to win the prize for which God has called me heavenward in Christ Jesus." No matter what your past looks like, you can choose a different path today.

Neither of my parents grew up in a Christ-centered home. Their heritage involved drunkenness, fighting, and fatherlessness. And yet they came together and chose to submit their lives and their home to Christ and to raise their children to fear the Lord. Though our family wasn't perfect, the Lord blessed the commitment of my parents. I've provided some statistics about how faith is best passed down from generation to generation. Maybe a godly, close-knit family is not your reality; but it can be your legacy. God's power and purposes exceed the bounds of statistics and data. He invites us to come to Him with willing hearts at any time, and He will step in with help and blessing. He is the One who restores, and He wants all people to come to saving faith in Him and experience abundant life. It's never too late to begin building better relationships where faith can flourish.

As we seek to transfer the beliefs and values we hold dear to the next generation, it's obvious that healthy relationships are a key ingredient. In cultivating strong bonds with the younger generation, we produce relationships that become fertile soil for planting seeds of faith. Strong, vibrant interpersonal connections are the secret to propagating faith that endures from generation to generation. Let's look at some of the characteristics of these relationships.

It's never too late
to begin building better
relationships where
faith can flourish.

———

Time. All relationships require time. At Generations Live, I encouraged women to slow down and spend time with God to grow their relationships with Him. The same is true with our children and those in our spheres of influence. We must slow down and be intentional to invest time in cultivating those relationships. Just as my relationship with my brother Ronald flourished because he sat and played dolls with me, my relationship with my children and grandchildren will flourish as we spend time together. Sometimes that requires participating in activities that aren't my preference but I do it because it is something important to my child.

As we carve out time to spend together, we should also be intentional. Four hours sitting in front of the TV together won't build connection the same way one hour of purposeful conversation will. We need to cultivate our family bonds in ways that allow our children to get to know us, as well as share and feel known.

Warmth. One study of three hundred families over thirty-five years revealed that family warmth was the top relational factor that correlated with transmission of faith. Commenting on these findings, *The Sticky Faith Guide for Your Family* reports, "Families in which parents and children felt close were more likely to be families in which children adopted the faith of their parents."[4]

This makes perfect sense because the Lord relates to us with warmth and kindness. He says, "Come to me, all you who are weary and burdened" (Matthew 11:28). He shelters us under His wing, He rejoices over us with singing. God goes out of His way to share a close, intimate relationship with us, and we must do the same with the next generation. Our children must feel that we love them and also like them. (There's a difference!) I believe my parents did a wonderful job of expressing warmth in the home that not only drew us in but also attracted other kids who maybe didn't have that warmth in their own homes. Young people have a keen sense of whether their presence is desired. Our homes should exude warmth and a sense of acceptance.

Meekness. Jesus said, "Blessed are the meek, for they will inherit the earth" (Matthew 5:5). Meekness is an underrated trait in our culture. One mistake some of us

---

4. Kara Powell, *The Sticky Faith Guide for Your Family: Over 100 Practical and Tested Ideas to Build Lasting Faith in Kids* (Grand Rapids, MI: Zondervan, 2014), 62.

in the older generation make is thinking our way is better and blasting that belief to our children. While we need to train those in the younger generation to respect their elders as Scripture commands, we must always remember we are still learning.

According to 2 Corinthians 3:18, "And we all, who with unveiled faces contemplate the Lord's glory, are being transformed into his image with ever-increasing glory, which comes from the Lord, who is the Spirit." We are *all* being transformed into his image with ever-increasing glory. None of us has arrived. Whether you're nine or ninety-nine, you're a work in progress. That's something I try to emphasize on the *Generations* show. The Lord can use anyone regardless of age to speak His wisdom and truth, and minister to others. As believers we can all learn from each other because the Spirit is at work in each of us.

Some of the most powerful moments growing up were the times when my mother or father asked me for forgiveness. I looked up to them, so when they humbled themselves to say, "I was wrong. Will you forgive me?" their words left a big impression. In those moments, they modeled meekness and gave me the opportunity to practice forgiveness and grace.

Fun. Science shows that we are wired for connection and empathy. One of the major ways we connect is through positive experiences and laughter. The Bible speaks of this in Proverbs 17:22: "A cheerful heart is good medicine, but a crushed spirit dries up the bones."

In my home growing up, my father was the king of fun. He went home to be with the Lord in 2009, but he is still one of the funniest people I have ever met. In addition to being funny, he was also caring. He kept his kids—and the neighborhood kids—busy with organized sports and games that were extremely competitive. There was always teasing and joking going on in our house.

My dad likely inherited some of his lively sense of humor from his mother, my Grandmother Howze. Jovial and full of wit, that woman could find humor in any situation. And she kept us laughing. One time, in a kind attempt to contribute to the practical needs of our large family, she bought an industrial-sized container of toilet paper. Clearly, she expected it to last for a while. But after only a few weeks, the toilet paper had disappeared.

"Y'all act like you have two butts apiece!" she exclaimed, hands on her hips and mouth agape. We laughed about that experience for years. Only having raised one child, my sweet grandmother had no idea how a family of twelve could go through toilet paper!

One of the things that first attracted me to my husband, Alvin, apart from his dashing good looks and warm smile, was his sense of humor. Not many people know this, but Alvin is very funny. Laughing together has kept our relationship going strong, even during stressful or heartbreaking seasons. When life gets heavy, a joyful heart is the good medicine we need. Because of this, we need to make levity a priority in our lives and homes.

Communication. Close relationships that transmit faith to the next generation require communication. Going back to Deuteronomy 6:7, we must talk to our kids about the ways of the Lord. But these conversations should happen naturally, not through preaching at them. For example, after watching a movie together, you could discuss how the movie reflects some truth about God or illuminates a pitfall we can face in life. At the dinner table, ask your child how she saw the Holy Spirit at work that day. As your kids are climbing into bed, debrief the day and pray over any concerns they may have.

If you don't have children in the home, you can still have these kinds of faith conversations with those in your circles. Meet for coffee and talk about what God is doing in each of your lives. Send prayers through text messages or write notes of encouragement containing Scripture. Even small communications can make a big impact.

CRAVING CONNECTION

We live in a world where people feel isolated and are craving a sense of connection. Social media occupies nearly 2.5 hours of that time.[5] You would think with all of this "connecting," we wouldn't be lonely anymore. But studies consistently show just the opposite—loneliness, friendlessness, and isolation are on the rise.

This is where the concept of generations can be so powerful. People of all ages can come together and find connection. We can invite the younger generation into the community God has provided through His people, which is how Christianity is meant to function. Even in its infancy, this community of Christ-followers was described this way:

---

5. Deyan G., "How Much Time Does the Average American Spend on Their Phone in 2022?," TechJury.net, June 3, 2022, https://techjury.net/blog/how-much-time-does-the-average-american-spend-on-their-phone/#gref; Brown, "Americans Spend Far More Time on Their Smartphones than They Think."

All the believers were together and had everything in common. They sold property and possessions to give to anyone who had need. Every day they continued to meet together in the temple courts. They broke bread in their homes and ate together with glad and sincere hearts, praising God and enjoying the favor of all the people. And the Lord added to their number daily those who were being saved. (Acts 2:44–47)

This passage has so many gems about how the family of God is to interact. But something to note is that these people did life together. They ate together, they sold their own possessions to care for the needy, they had glad hearts (fun!), and they praised God together. And the people around them weren't looking on with distain at these weird Christians. No, they wanted in on it! The believers enjoyed the favor of all people, and the Lord added daily to their number.

That is the kind of connection and belonging we need to extend to the next generation. It's something so much richer than what they will find at the bar or in the club or on their phones. Our homes and churches should offer acceptance, encouragement, and fun. Christian relationships should be the best relationships because Christ is at their core. Faith in Jesus breaks down barriers, including those that separate generations. As we praise the Lord together and welcome in new believers, we offer an oasis of joy, fellowship, and peace amid a hectic, divided, lonely world. But cultivating these strong relationships takes time and effort.

MAKING TOUGH CHOICES

When people ask me what I did to have strong relationships with my grown children, I say, "I fought for it." It wasn't always easy. Sometimes I had to make difficult choices to protect those relationships. When my children were young, my music career was flourishing. I was regularly invited to give concerts, sing at award ceremonies, and even tour overseas. Something that helped me balance my family relationships with my work was identifying my priorities. My relationship with God was my top priority. Next came my relationship with my husband, Alvin. Next on the list were my children, followed by ministry and career.

I had to establish my priorities early in my career so that I wouldn't be pulled away by things of lesser importance. When I was invited to tour overseas, I had to put a cap on the time I would spend away from home. I always insisted on catching a red-eye flight home after an award ceremony was over. In my 1999 memoir, *On a Positive Note*, I wrote, "I know firsthand how easy it is to become so drunk by this carousel called stardom, so dazed by your own ambitions, hungry for the next conquest, that you lose sight of what's really important. Christians can get so caught up in the business that they can neglect their spiritual needs. When that happens, we become vulnerable."[6]

The wonderful thing is, when you make God your priority, He backs you up. He always blesses those tough choices that swing in favor of His will for you. When our young family moved from Detroit to Nashville it was a bit of a shock. In my hometown of Detroit, I always had more than enough babysitters for my children because my family and friends lived there. Moving to Nashville meant losing my godly, trusted help.

I remember praying and asking the Lord to bring me the help I needed to continue to answer the call He had on my life, both in my family obligations and my music career. He was faithful to do exactly that. He blessed us with a great church to attend and get connected. He also brought into my life an incredible young woman named Chandra. She loved God and my children.

---

6. Winans, *On a Positive Note*, 128.

When Alvin III and Ashley were in their preteen years, they had a high need for their father and me to pour into their lives. My record label wanted me to go on tour, and I knew I couldn't leave my kids for an extended period. I sought the Lord in prayer and told Him that if He wanted me to go on tour, He would have to provide a way. And that's exactly what He did.

Chandra offered to travel with us and homeschool Alvin and Ashley on the road. After some prayer, my husband and I felt a peace about pulling our children out of school and going on the road together. We only did this for a few years, but the experience provided many sweet memories. An added benefit of this adventure was that my children were able to have a front-row seat to see how God was using their mom and dad to bless and serve others.

In that instance, when I was confronted with a career opportunity that conflicted with my priorities, I asked God to provide a solution. If He hadn't made a way, I was willing to make the tough choice to stay home. (Although if you know me, you know it wouldn't have been *too* tough, because I love staying home.) Many times, I think we get caught up in committing to "good" things without reviewing our priorities and allowing them to dictate our choices. One way we can fight for strong relationships is by making sure we consult the Lord on our daily choices and honor the priorities we believe He's given us.

Another way I fought for a good relationship with my children was by taking my assignment as a mother seriously. I understood my job was to train my children in the Lord and raise them to know His ways, not be their best friend. Sometimes this meant my decisions as their mother weren't popular.

When they were young, I put Alvin and Ashley in dance lessons with some of their friends. One day, when I went and watched the class, I didn't feel good about what I saw. Some of the dance moves were suggestive, and a few of the song lyrics were questionable. I had the gut check from the Holy Spirit, big time. Even though some of their Christian friends were in the class, I pulled them out. Alvin and Ashley were angry. They were good dancers and enjoyed the class. But I knew the Lord was guiding me in my decision, so I stuck with it. And looking back I can see the wisdom in that decision.

As my children grew and I continued to press in, they began to better understand and appreciate my role in their lives. They understood that I wanted what was best for them, and the discipline, care, and attention I gave them deepened our relationship. We still had some bad days, and when we did, I would call my mother or the older ladies at my church and glean from their parenting wisdom. They would encourage me, give advice, point me to God's Word, and remind me that I was not alone in my parenting struggles.

From what I observe, too many parents pull back from a relationship with their children when they should be pressing in. I remember times when I would be on my knees before the Lord praying for one of my children and the Holy Spirit would tell me, "Go to their room!" I would knock on the door and say, "We need to talk." My children didn't always welcome my intrusion, but these drop-in conversations built closeness and ultimately strengthened our relationship.

Over time I learned not only to pray for my concerns for my children, but also to thank God for His good plans for them. When my kids were in their teen years, I attended a conference where I heard about the power of confession. I learned that as I prayed, I could thank God for the things I wanted Him to do in my children's life. I could pray, "Thank you, Lord, that you have made Ashley to be a woman of valor and godly character, someone who seeks You in everything she does." Regardless of whether I saw these things in my daughter or not, I could confess them, knowing that they were in accordance with the will of God.

One day I tested it out as I was speaking with Alvin III when he was sixteen. As he was growing into a young man, my son had become a person I didn't fully understand or even recognize. On one level this was terrifying, but I was also determined not to give him too much space as he developed into his own person. That day during an argument, I blurted out, "Alvin, you are a mighty man of God!"

He stopped arguing and looked at me quizzically. "You don't even believe that yourself," he said.

And he was right! But I didn't let him know that. My words had caught my son's attention. He had heard my proclamation of his godly character. In the days and months that followed, I continued to thank the Lord that Alvin was a mighty man of God who would use every talent he'd been given for God's glory. Alvin still had some things to wrestle through before he would fully walk in that calling, but today he is my pastor, and he is using every one of his gifts to honor God when shepherding His people. I'm so grateful I continued to push him toward the Lord instead of backing away.

BUILDING BETTER RELATIONSHIPS

President Theodore Roosevelt famously said, "People don't care how much you know until they know how much you care." Those are apt words when it comes to instructing the next generation in the ways of the Lord. We can teach our children the precepts of God until we are blue in the face, but without relationship and proven love, our words will fall flat.

Maybe as you've read this chapter you feel as if you've missed the window of opportunity. Perhaps your children are grown, and you regret that you don't share a close relationship. One of the reasons I began the *Generations* show was to encourage people that it's never too late to strengthen intergenerational bonds.

There's always hope. Pray now, like you should have prayed then. Invest the time now, like you should have invested it then. Ask the Lord how to bring closeness to those relationships. James 1:5 says, "If any of you lacks wisdom, you should ask God, who gives generously to all without finding fault, and it will be given to you." Ask God for wisdom as you rebuild or build for the first time those vital relationships. The Holy Spirit knows how to penetrate hearts and restore broken bonds. It's never too late. No matter how many years you feel you've missed out on, the Holy Spirit can make up for that time.

And if you still have children in the home, fight for those relationships. Fight in prayer. Fight by making tough choices that align with your priorities. Fight by understanding your assignment to pass down the faith. Fight by pressing in and confessing the faith and godliness you desire to see. Don't give up. And as you fight, remember that God goes with you into the battle and He wins the victory.

QUESTIONS *to* CONSIDER

- What is the story you received from your family of origin? How has this shaped what you're passing on to the next generation?

  _____

  _____

  _____

- What aspects of strong relationships do you need to concentrate on the most? (For example, time, warmth, humility, fun, communication, and so on.)

  _____

  _____

  _____

- Take some time to ask the Holy Spirit to give you wisdom on how to strengthen your relationships.

  _____

  _____

  _____

CHAPTER

·eight·

FACING ADVERSITY

Everyone experiences storms in life. One of my biggest storms was losing my brother Ronald. In 1997, my brother Marvin took Ronald, who was coughing and experiencing shortness of breath, to the doctor. It's still a mystery how Ronald was able to walk into the hospital that day. The physicians discovered that Ronald had suffered a major heart attack several months earlier and would need immediate surgery. His heart, which should have been the size of a closed fist, was so enlarged it filled his entire chest cavity. Even with surgery, the prognosis wasn't good.

On a plane from Salt Lake City to Detroit I felt so fearful. "Not now, Lord," I prayed. "Not Ronald." The entire family gathered at the hospital to pray for a miracle and plead for Ronald's life. At one point the surgeon came in and told us there was nothing more he could do for Ronald. His heart refused to beat on its own apart from the bypass machine. We asked the doctor if we could pray for *him*, and he agreed. After a powerful time of prayer for that surgeon, my dad took his hands and said, "Go back and take my son off that machine. He will live."

And my dad was right. When the doctor weaned Ronald off the bypass machine, his heart miraculously began beating on its own. God had answered our prayers and saved Ronald's life. Once he had recuperated, he went right back to performing with my brothers and shared his gift of music and his testimony with thousands of people.

Maybe that's why his death on June 17, 2005, took me by surprise. After the miracle God had given us, Ronald was supposed to live a long life, not leave us at forty-eight due to heart complications. My dad, on the other hand, lifted his hands and praised the Lord when my brother had taken his last breath. My dad had a deep, abiding faith, and he was willing to accept the Lord's will and praise even in grief.

Earlier that year, I had joined Ronald on stage at Greater Grace Temple to sing "My Help (Cometh from the Lord)" as part of his Family and Friends Celebration concert, which would be his last recording. As part of the concert, the surgeon who had operated on my brother in 1997 came on stage and shared his testimony about what God had done for us that day. He testified that none of his colleagues had believed that Ronald would live and that God had truly done a miracle.

A few minutes later, when I joined Ronald on stage, he beamed with pride as he introduced me in his genteel manner: "Ladies and gentlemen, my sister CeCe." With nearly a hundred singers backing us up, our impassioned duet electrified the large auditorium. It felt like home to be singing with my big brother and our other siblings as we had done since we were children. Each of us was unique and had struck out on our own paths in both life and music, but we shared the bond of growing up in the Winans family, reared on songs of praise since childhood. There's nothing quite like singing with my siblings. It's as if each note calls back a memory of sitting next to one another in the church pew or standing around the family piano, singing our favorite gospel songs. That feeling of joy and exhilaration must be a little bit like what heaven will feel like. And that day, I didn't know just how close my brother was to meeting Jesus face to face.

I was on tour when I learned that Ronald had passed after a short stay in the hospital. I was devastated. My Ronald, the gentle teenage boy who had played dolls with his little sister. The big teddy bear of a man, whose comforting embrace could bring peace to any situation. The one who was my protector and always looked out for everyone in our family.

Just after my brother died, I remember talking to my sister Debbie. "CeCe, how are we gonna make it?" she asked.

"I don't know," I replied. "All I know is we serve a God who's faithful and knows how we're going to make it."

Ronald was the first of our family members to graduate to heaven, and our hearts were broken. Losing him was the most difficult thing I've ever endured, the closest I've come to having my spirit crushed. Though I never considered giving up my faith, my faith was tested. James tells us that the testing of our faith produces perseverance that we may be mature, complete, not lacking anything (1:3–4). But losing Ronald at such a young age would never have been my plan. His loss left a deep hole, not only in our family but in the gospel music world. I had to trust that God's ways were best. I had to praise Him for saving my brother eight years earlier *and* for sovereignly taking him home at his appointed time.

PRAISING IN THE DARK

When tragedy or hardship comes, holding onto belief can be difficult because we can't always see how God is working. Part of being a Christian is believing in the character of God and the promises of God even when we cannot see. Scripture reminds us, "We live by faith, not by sight" (2 Corinthians 5:7). This kind of faith is so critical because Jesus told us that in this world we would have trouble.

In the quest to pass on faith to the next generation, we will encounter challenges and adversity. These may be related to our mission—for example, having a child who is not walking with the Lord or is struggling with addiction or mental illness. Or the adversity may fall into the category of general trials, such as the loss of a loved one, illness, a job loss, or divorce. These kinds of troubles, though not specifically related to our mission of passing on faith, can still distract and even derail us from our calling.

When Ronald first left us, I was not sure how I could continue giving concerts and encouraging others when I was grieving so deeply. Standing on stage one night a few weeks after he'd passed away, I asked the Lord, "How am I going to do this?" I felt His Holy Spirit sustaining me as I began to sing "He's Concerned," a song that was in my regular lineup. I could hardly believe the lyrics:

God is just a prayer away.
All you need to do is call.
He will hear your faintest cry.
He's concerned about you.
So while your tears are flowing through, your
    time of mourning,
He is here to lift your heavy heart, 'cause He is
    in love with you.

The words of a song I had sung hundreds of times ministered to me so deeply. It reminded me that the Lord saw me and He cared. He was not surprised by Ronald's departure to glory. God loved me and was just a prayer away. The prayers of saints from around the world added to my comfort.

At Ronald's memorial service, Bishop Norman Wagner said to us, "There are going to be some days when you don't feel like you have the strength to do what you need to do. I want you to know you don't have to have it because we're praying for you. We're stepping in and holding up your arms." Bishop Wagner was referring to the Old Testament story in which Aaron and Hur lift Moses's tired arms to help the Israelites prevail in battle (Exodus 17:12). It's a powerful picture of how we can support one another through difficulties.

The prayers of God's people have carried me through so many storms in life. In moments of tragedy, hardship, and suffering, you need your brothers and sisters. In my life, God has used them to comfort me, pray for me, encourage me, and ease my burden. My dear friend, Whitney Houston, was one of the people who came to Ronald's service to support me. Whitney and I had met early in our careers, and she had proven to be a faithful friend. Not only did we talk regularly on the phone, but I had also become godmother to her daughter, Bobbi Kristina Brown. In 1996 we recorded the song "Count on Me" for the movie *Waiting to Exhale*. The song, which talked about leaning on one another during hard times and being strong when the other is weak, was a perfect fit for us and struck a chord with listeners, rising to number eight on the charts.

Although she was a superstar, Whitney was always there for me when I needed her, and her presence at

Ronald's funeral was a great comfort to me. In 2022, I dedicated an episode of the *Generations* show to my friend. We honored her memory by talking with her brother and sister-in-law about the wonderful, gifted, and genuine person she was. It was friends like Whitney and so many others in the body of Christ who lifted me up when I was going through the sorrow of losing my brother. God revealed His love and care for me through the comfort of my community.

STAYING ON COURSE

We must expect adversity in this life. Something I've realized is that often what we do *before* the trial comes is just as important as what we do after. When Jesus was on earth, He told a parable about a wise man and a foolish man.

> Therefore everyone who hears these words of mine and puts them into practice is like a wise man who built his house on the rock. The rain came down, the streams rose, and the winds blew and beat against that house; yet it did not fall, because it had its foundation on the rock. But everyone who hears these words of mine and

does not put them into practice is like a foolish man who built his house on sand. The rain came down, the streams rose, and the winds blew and beat against that house, and it fell with a great crash. (Matthew 7:24–27)

Jesus's story isn't about the builder, what the houses looked like, or even the materials the structures were made of. It's all about *where* the house was built and what it was built upon. The one who hears Jesus's words and puts them into practice is like the one who built his house on a rock—a safe, secure location when bad weather comes. The one who hears Jesus's words and does not put them into practice is like the one who built his house on the sand—a dangerous, unstable spot when bad weather comes.

Both individuals heard Jesus's words. The difference was in their response. The wise man heard the words and put them into practice, while the foolish man heard the words and did not put them into practice. Building our lives on the rock involves action. Hearing the words is not enough; we must respond in obedience by doing what God says. This is shown through our spiritual rhythms, the patterns we incorporate into our daily lives.

Here's the thing. Bad weather always comes. No one gets through life without some adversity. The best way to ensure the house stands is by building our lives on the rock of Jesus Christ. We do this by establishing during the good times healthy patterns that endure when times get tough. When the foundation of our lives is grounded in the words and ways of Christ, the storms of life don't destroy us.

When I lost my brother, the grief knocked the wind out of me. I had to walk in what I knew—those disciplines of prayer, trust, being in the Word, and calling on others to pray. I reminded Him of His promises. "You promised me peace," I told the Lord. "You promised me strength. You promised me hope." The enemy couldn't take the truths of God from me, because I had diligently stored them in my heart since I was a girl. Our enemy doesn't always steal from us in big ways. In fact, his most crafty work is winning little victories, such as convincing us we don't have time to read God's Word or that church isn't that important. Then when something big comes, you don't have the stamina to walk through it. The everyday disciplines build you up so you can persevere through trials.

That's why it's so important to be consistent in your walk with God, spending time in His Word and in prayer, fellowshipping with other believers, and depending on His Holy Spirit. Every quiet time may not be earth shattering. Sometimes you will feel refreshed and transformed, and other times you may not. But what you do today is stored up for future days. When adversity comes, you're not wondering what to do. When the rain comes down and the streams rise and the wind beats against the house, that house of your life stands. And the more you do these things in good times and bad, the more you will trust God. I can look back over my life and see that in the hardest times with my children, in my marriage, and with my family, God never failed. When people failed, He never did.

I don't know if life is good for you right now or if you're being tossed around in the storms of life. I do know that the God of the universe is more powerful than any storm. The reason I know is not only because God's Word says so, but because I have personally experienced it. In the words of the old hymn "My Hope Is Built on Nothing Less," "In every high and stormy gale, my anchor holds within the veil. On Christ the solid rock I stand. All other

In every high
and stormy gale, my
anchor holds within
the veil. On Christ the
solid rock I stand.

ground is sinking sand." As I have put His words into practice, Christ has been my solid rock.

More than that, He is a tender companion when we go through suffering. Many of us experienced loss during the coronavirus pandemic. From stay-at-home orders to quarantines to health crises, we've all lost experiences, familiar rhythms, relationships, opportunities, and peace of mind. Those kinds of losses take a toll and result in collective grief. We may have moved forward, but the effects are still evident in the world around us. Many of us are hurting from those circumstances or others. As a Christian, I *know* "I can do all things through him who gives me strength" (Philiphians 4:13). The problem arises when I skip the lament and attempt to jump straight to the joy in my own strength.

When we're going through a trying season, we may also forget how intensely our Savior cares for us in our lowest moments. He sits with us in our pain. When Jesus's friend Lazarus died, Jesus wept with Mary and Martha mere moments before He brought their brother back to life. Jesus knew the joy that awaited the women, and still He cried with them. I find that incredible. That is the kind of Savior we have. He sees our pain, understands it, and cares.

Whenever we lament—whether over a broken relationship, medical diagnosis, or heartbreaking loss—Jesus, the "man of sorrows," is right there with us. He knows when and how healing and restoration will occur, but He also sits with us in our pain. He invites us to bring our sorrow to Him and allow His Spirit to turn it to joy.

THE POWER OF PRAISE

As a girl, I witnessed the power of praise firsthand. Rain or shine, my dad was always praising Jesus. He didn't care how loud he was or where he was. He had only to think on the goodness of God, and praise would flow out. At times this could be surprising, like when it happened in the line at a department store. "We thank you, Jesus!" he would exclaim. "Lord, you are so good!"

My mother also kept praise on her lips, though she was less boisterous about it. Whether she received good news or bad, I would hear her say, "Lord, we bless your name." I never doubted how my mom or dad felt about the Lord or how deeply they trusted Him.

I inherited the practice of praise from my parents. One day, when my children were in elementary school, I realized just how much my habit of praising God out loud had impacted them. While I was out of town, they made me a video of part of their day. As they climbed into the car for school, Ashley, pretending to be me, raised her hand and said, "Oh God, we bless Your name."

"God, You are so good!" Alvin III chimed in.

I smiled, both at their amusing impersonation of their mother and at the fact that they had picked up on my inclination to praise. Psalm 34:1–2 says, "I will extol the LORD at all times; his praise will always be on my lips. I will glory in the LORD; let the afflicted hear and rejoice." Praise is an antidote to affliction. When I have walked through hard times in my life, praise has been a proven path to victory. As we praise, God becomes bigger and our problems become smaller. Here are a few times Scripture commands us to praise.

In the morning. Multiple Scriptures tell us to praise God first thing in the morning. This helps us gain the proper perspective before we begin our day. One morning I was doing devotions with my grandson, Wyatt, and we read Psalm 59:16: "But I will sing of your strength, in the morning I will sing of your love; for you are my fortress, my refuge in times of trouble."

"Oooo, Wyatt," I said. "That's what we do. We sing praise to God in the morning! We remember He is our fortress." I turned on some kids worship music, filling the room with praise. As he started dancing and praising

God, I was reminded of the importance of praising God throughout my day. As I do, my family and those around me are affected by my praise. At Nashville Life, I'll often come in Sunday morning with praise on my lips, and some of our young congregants have started imitating this kind of spontaneous worship.

When we're in need. The Word says that God is present in the praises of His people. And Philippians 4:6 tells us, "Do not be anxious about anything, but in every situation, by prayer and petition, with thanksgiving, present your requests to God." You start with giving thanks to God and remembering who He is. You make your requests with thanksgiving, proclaiming that He is big enough, wise enough, and good enough to handle any problem in your life.

I think of Paul and Silas, imprisoned for preaching the gospel. After receiving a severe beating, the two evangelists sat, their feet in stocks, in the inner cell of the jail. Scripture tells us how they responded to this hardship: "About midnight Paul and Silas were praying and singing hymns to God, and the other prisoners were listening to them. Suddenly there was such a violent earthquake that the foundations of the prison were shaken. At once all the prison doors flew open, and everyone's chains came loose" (Acts 16:25–26).

Reading on, we discover that when this miracle occurs, Paul and Silas don't seize their opportunity to escape prison, but instead witness to the jailer, who comes to saving faith in Christ. The men praised God through their hardship, and as a result, God brought about something far greater than their immediate rescue.

As an example to others. Earlier in this book, we examined Psalm 145:4–7, which talks about influencing the next generation:

> One generation commends your works to another;
>> they tell of your mighty acts.
> They speak of the glorious splendor of your
>> majesty—
>> and I will meditate on your wonderful works.
> They tell of the power of your awesome works—
>> and I will proclaim your great deeds.
> They celebrate your abundant goodness
>> and joyfully sing of your righteousness.

The focus of this entire passage is praise. We don't just teach our children about God, we praise His works to them. We talk about how good He is, we speak of His mighty acts, we sing of His righteousness, and we celebrate His goodness. As odd as my father's outbursts of praise may have seemed in the moment, he was doing this 100 percent! We could see that God was number one in his life. He always testified of God's goodness and worthiness.

We must be lifting up God's name and magnifying Him so the next generation understands this is not a boring religion or a passionless daily grind; it's an exciting walk with God. We must broadcast that we believe God is bigger than our problems. We praise Him according to his excellence, not what our feelings or circumstances dictate.

WHO DO YOU WORSHIP?

We are created to worship. Praising God has helped me to overcome adversity in my life. Praise is one of our greatest weapons against the attacks of the enemy. Praise brings in the light and keeps you from dwelling on darkness. As you worship, you're not denying the reality of whatever difficult circumstance you're walking through. But praise shifts your focus from the problem to the answer, from the mountain to the mountain mover. It reminds you of the glorious truths that you are more than a conqueror, God is for you, and greater is He who is in you than he who is in the world. Praise allows the Holy Spirit to move and work in ways that proclaim the glory of God even in the direst circumstances.

At Ronald's memorial service, I declared as part of my tribute that we were "choosing to take on a garment of praise for any and all potential spirits of heaviness." Because we chose to praise, the service was filled with laughter, love, and honor of my brother, a man whose legacy would long outlive him.

At my brother's memorial, I said,

Ronald passing twice changed my life forever twice. The first time when God brought him back my faith went somewhere it never went before because when you witness God bring back someone from the dead, you know He can work out anything. This time when he passed, I changed again. My mind went straight to heaven and I'm so focused to live for God like never before, and I've realized there is nothing else more important than loving God and loving each other.

The surgeon who had operated on Ronald in 1997 also spoke. Holding back tears, he talked about the surgery he'd performed on my brother nearly eight years earlier. He said, "Ron helped bring me back to God after

I walked away from Him, thinking that it was me who was responsible for the patients I helped, when the reality is it was God." After experiencing the miracle God did for Ronald, that doctor turned back to the Lord, offering Him all praise for what He had done.

God had used tragedy to point our eyes toward heaven and to His eternal purposes. Ronald brought people to the Lord both in life and in death. That evening the Lord was present in the praises of His people. We declared His mighty acts in and through the life of our brother and friend Ronald. I would never be the same. But I would keep building my life on the rock of Jesus as my brother had done. Because one day, I will see them both face to face.

- What is a trial you have experienced in the past or are currently experiencing? What impact has it had on your life?

  _____

  _____

- What spiritual disciplines or practices have strengthened you in times of adversity?

  _____

  _____

- How does it make you feel that Jesus cares about you enough to enter your suffering?

  _____

  _____

- Have you experienced the power of praise in your life? What happened?

  _____

  _____

PASSING THE BATON

When God called Alvin and me to pastor Nashville Life Church in 2012, He revealed to my husband that our son, Alvin III, would be our successor. So we knew from the start our leadership of the church was temporary. We had been pastoring for eight years when my husband felt the prompt from the Holy Spirit that the time for the handoff was near. From my perspective, my son did not look ready. He was only thirty-five years old, and though he had been serving in a pastoral role from the start of Nashville Life, I wondered if he was ready to take on the rigors and responsibilities of lead pastor.

In addition, the timing felt strange. We were in the middle of a global pandemic with social, racial, and political unrest in the culture that was also affecting our church. Alvin III would have to lead our very diverse congregation during arguably one of the toughest times to be a pastor. At the time, the church was doing well and there was no obvious reason to change up the leadership, but our instructions from the Lord had been clear. He had stirred in my husband's heart that the timing was right.

So at the end of 2020, we began taking the steps necessary to officially hand over the lead pastor duties to Alvin III at the start of the new year. Since the Lord had taken hold of our son's life nearly fifteen years earlier, I had watched Him develop some beautiful leadership qualities in Alvin. We decided to seek help with the transition, we had already hired a coach several years earlier to come alongside us during the handoff. We wanted the process to be as seamless as possible. Our top priority was not to disrupt the work God was doing at the church.

"You're going to have to allow him to drop the ball sometimes," the coach warned us during one of our first meetings.

"Why?" I asked, my mother's heart fretting for my son. "Can't we just catch the balls for him?"

"No," he told us. "You have to step back. He's watched you two do it. You have taught him. You have raised him. Now you have to take your hands off."

We learned that sometimes when churches go through a leadership change, the previous pastor is asked to leave for at least six months to allow the new leadership to take. But after seeking the Lord on the matter, Alvin and I felt strongly that God was calling us to stick around to visibly show support for our son in his new role. The coach assured us that Alvin would make mistakes. "But I'm here to help him," he said, "and it's going to be okay."

It's going to be okay. Those words can be so hard to believe sometimes. The enemy is intent on stealing our peace. Even though Alvin and I knew it was God's will to pass the leadership of the church to Alvin III, the exact details of how to do it weren't written down for us in Scripture. There wasn't an exact blueprint. It was going to be a little messy. Something that reassured me was that Jesus never ran away from the mess. He walked through it. He sat in it. He ministered to the mess.

If I ask my one-year-old grandson, Wyatt, to come help me clean up a mess, I can expect things to get worse before they get better. There will be times when I'll think, *I'd just rather do this myself because I can get it done quickly.* But if I ask him to help and allow him to make the mess he's going to make, he's learning the principles and the work ethic to eventually do the task on his own with excellence.

God was asking us to hand something over to someone who might not do the job to our exact standard. We had to trust that He had called our son to the task. First Thessalonians 5:24 says, "The one who calls you is faithful, and he will do it." The Lord had called Alvin III to be our lead pastor, and He would do it. Our job was to hand over the task with grace and get out of the way.

WHO ARE YOU TEACHING?

The story of Paul and Timothy is a classic example of spiritual mentorship. Paul, who referred to the young pastor as "my true son in the faith," shared a close connection with Timothy (2 Timothy 1:2). In 2 Timothy 1:5–7 we observe a powerful mentorship moment:

> I am reminded of your sincere faith, which first lived in your grandmother Lois and in your mother Eunice and, I am persuaded, now lives in you also. For this reason I remind you to fan into flame the gift of God, which is in you through the laying on of my hands. For the Spirit God gave us does not make us timid, but gives us power, love and self-discipline.

Several things stand out to me in this passage. First, Paul knows Timothy's history. Although he's not physically related to Timothy, he acknowledges that the young man's grandmother Lois and his mother, Eunice, have passed down the faith to him. This passage offers me inspiration for obvious reasons. As a mother and a grandmother, my role in passing down the faith matters. Also, you don't have to be related by blood to have a spiritual influence on someone's life. Many of us may be a spiritual mother or father to someone. In knowing who Timothy is, Paul can remind him of the faith that has been growing in him since childhood. I have been encouraged in this way many times throughout my life.

The second thing I notice in this passage is that Paul encourages Timothy in his specific gifts and calling. The apostle has firsthand knowledge of Timothy's spiritual gifts, and he encourages the young man to step into them more fully. This is what my husband, Alvin, and I needed to do with our son. God was calling us to empower Alvin III to step into his gifts and be our lead pastor. In addition to reminding Timothy of his gift, Paul reminds the young pastor that God's Spirit will give him the boldness, power, and love to step into his calling. In doing this, he points Timothy to his true source of strength and help.

You don't have to
be related by blood to
have a spiritual influence
on someone's life.

———————

In the next chapter, Paul charges Timothy with the important task of passing down faith to others: "You then, my son, be strong in the grace that is in Christ Jesus. And the things you have heard me say in the presence of many witnesses entrust to reliable people who will also be qualified to teach others" (2 Timothy 2:1–2). With these instructions, Paul lays out a model for multigenerational disciple-making. He invites Timothy to take what he has learned and pass it on to faithful people who are then able to teach others. Bringing this principle to my own experience—I pass the spiritual wisdom that my mom and dad entrusted to me to my children so that they may teach the next generation.

This is an exciting task but not always easy to execute. Part of the problem comes in the form of generational conflict. This tension happens when the interests or ideals of one generation clash with those of another—for example, a baby boomer believing a millennial is lazy or entitled. While there are many varieties of individuals within each generation—typically those born within a twenty-year period—each individual shares similarities in behavior, philosophy, and attitude, as well as a sense of common identity. Like gender, race, or nationality, age is one more social dynamic that can divide us and cause us to be distrustful of those not in our own camp.

Perhaps this is the reason so many churches struggle to retain the young people in their congregations. As Alvin and I discovered firsthand, millennials (those born between 1981 and 1996) have struggled to find their place in the church. But one study reports that 45 percent of Gen Z Americans (those born in 1997 or after) rarely or never attend church, with one in four attending weekly or more.[1]

And the younger generations aren't the only ones whose church attendance is flagging. Church attendance patterns reveal that baby boomers and Gen Xers are just as likely to stop attending church as millennials and Gen Zers.[2] Not only are these statistics heartbreaking, but they also show a generational breakdown. Instead of the discipleship flow Paul describes, churchgoers are failing to plug in, get discipled, and, in turn, disciple others.

I see a big opportunity here, which is why I started *Generations.* We need to bring people together from all generations and start a conversation so that we can effectively

---

1. Melissa Deckman, "Generation Z and Religion: What New Data Show," Religion in Public, February 10, 2020, https://religioninpublic.blog/2020/02/10/generation-z-and-religion-what-new-data-show/.
2. Adam MacInnis, "The Church Is Losing Its Gray Heads," *Christianity Today*, February 14, 2022, www.christianitytoday.com/ct/2022/march/gray-gen-x-boomers-older-churchgoers-leaving-church.html.

pass on faith the way God intended. We are better together than we are apart. This phrase can apply to many arenas, but I believe intergenerational relationships is one of them.

In His wisdom, God invented the concept of generations. He knew that they would each be different, shaped by their cultural surroundings and the significant events of their times. God sent His Son into a specific culture, a specific mix of generations. Jesus was raised and reared by a mother and father, whom He honored. Because of His radical message, He experienced conflict with the established religious leaders, many of whom were likely from the older generation. And He chose disciples to pour into from among the young and inexperienced. Jesus preached that His Father's kingdom was equal opportunity. He welcomed the children, the elderly, and every age in between to be saved and participate in this kingdom.

The gospel transcends generational divides. It connects us all under one banner of faith in Christ. We must be strategic in rejecting the world's view on generations or practicing ageism. Other age groups are not our enemies. In fact, they can be our greatest assets. The Bible instructs believers to live at peace and in unity with one another so that the world may see God through them. To do this, younger generations must learn to show honor to their elders. Those of us who are older must learn to trust those younger than ourselves so we are able to *entrust* the gospel message and oversight of the church to their care. As we seek to bridge the generational divide, here are a few things to consider.

We are commanded to show honor. We have a crisis of honor in our culture. Children don't honor their parents. We don't honor our elders. We don't honor the governing authorities God has placed over us. Scripture tells us that unity demands a blessing (Psalm 133:1–3). To have unity, you must have regard and deference for others. When I look around at this world, I see that we do a very poor job at showing honor to our fellow humankind.

Not long ago, John Bevere spoke at our church on what it means to honor each other. By the halfway point of his message, I was openly repenting. He told a story about going through the TSA line at the airport, a travel requirement many, including myself, find frustrating. Even though TSA workers may be viewed as an annoyance to many of us, John said, they are doing their job for our safety and they deserve honor for that.

"That day, I stopped in the middle of the security line, and told a worker, 'Thank you for what you do,'" John said. "I showed him honor."

The TSA attendant seemed taken aback but responded, "Thank you so much."

After John shared that story, I yelled, "I repent, Lord!"

John laughed, but I was so convicted by his powerful message. We are all created in God's image, and Jesus shed His precious blood to purchase salvation for all who believe. Each human God created deserves honor. I cannot honor God if I refuse to honor the people He created and loves. As believers, we should be leading the way in showing honor. As 1 Peter 4:17 says so powerfully, "For the time has come for judgment to begin at the house of God" (NKJV). As Christ-followers, we can't allow a culture of dishonor to shape us; we must shape the culture by outdoing one another in showing honor as Romans 12:10 instructs.

I intentionally began by reminding us that the command to honor is for every person regardless of age. Sometimes we view this going one direction, as in the younger generation honoring the older. I grew up with a strong respect for my elders. I never called adults by their first names. I addressed adults in my life with "Yes, sir" and "Yes, ma'am," and I honored my parents.

Ephesians 6:2–3 says, "'Honor your father and mother'—which is the first commandment with a promise—'so that it may go well with you and that you may enjoy long life on the earth.'" I grew up knowing this commandment and promise and following it. And I see how honoring my parents, as they also honored their parents, has brought blessing in my life.

When Alvin and I began working with young people at church, we discovered that this issue of honoring one's parents could be complicated. Some of our congregants had parents who weren't believers or had hurt them in some way. We explained that you don't have to agree with your parents to honor them in a biblical way. You don't have to believe the same things or even have a good relationship. Honoring is showing respect because that person is created by God and holds a God-given role in your life. They may have parented imperfectly, but you can choose to show them the basic respect their position demands, while maintaining healthy boundaries.

Honoring my parents and submitting to godly authority in my life is something God has used to guide and protect me. God's ways are always set up for our good. God's Word contains many promises about the benefits of obedience in this area of honor. As we walk it out, He pours out blessing, peace, wisdom, and protection in our lives.

When Alvin and I were dating, I went to Pastor Stacks, my pastor at the time, to get his blessing. At nineteen I knew I needed to have my parents and spiritual leaders on board with my choice of a spouse. Pastor Stacks took my request seriously and asked that Alvin and I separate and not talk to each other for a certain number of days while he prayed about the matter.

A few weeks later, Pastor Stacks called me, and I was delighted to hear his assessment. "You've got a good guy," he said. "He loves God more than he loves you." I cannot tell you how much peace and comfort it gave me to know that my pastor had sought the Lord and approved of my marriage to Alvin. During the rough times in our marriage—and we've had some—I could always go back to that moment when I submitted to my spiritual authorities. It gave me the strength to endure, knowing that God had confirmed our marriage through multiple people who were seeking Him and whom we respected.

As I've already mentioned, honor and respect go both ways. Those of us in the older generation need to honor our younger brothers and sisters as individuals who possess wisdom and a fresh perspective. Instead of engaging in the age-old "kids these days" critique, we're in a unique position to respect the younger generation and, in doing so, call the best out of them.

We are called to train our replacements. No matter your age, there will come a time when you can't do the things you're doing today. And that switch can happen fast. Instead of clutching leadership until the last possible moment, we should be actively building into our future leaders. That's why my husband and I decided to hand the lead pastor role to Alvin III, at the Lord's prompting, even though we were still capable of leading and were seeing fruit in our ministry. We wanted to allow him to grow into the position while we were still around to support him and be a resource.

Unfortunately, the older generation isn't always willing to pass down the ministries God has given them until forced to do so. To use the analogy of passing the baton, instead of a graceful handoff, they clutch the baton until they are forced to drop it (or it's ripped out of their hands). When we pass on the faith in this manner, we miss out on the joys and benefits of truly investing in those who will carry the mantle when our race has come to an end. We get to be part of the "cloud of witnesses" who cheer on devoted faith in the next generation (Hebrews 12:1). As we set them up for success, we can play a key role in helping them get off the blocks quickly in their own race of faith.

One challenge we may face in trying to pass the baton is when the younger generation doesn't seem to want what we're trying to impart. Because of relational breakdown between generations, this does happen frequently in my experience. Instead of being receptive to mentorship from someone older and wiser, young leaders might think they have it all figured out and be resistant to help. They may give the impression that the old regime is irrelevant or that you have nothing to offer them.

While it's demoralizing to receive this reaction, we are not responsible for someone else's response. We're responsible for telling the story about God's faithfulness and greatness. Don't be discouraged. Even the people in Jesus's hometown rejected Him. Listen to His response: "A prophet is not without honor except in his own town and in his own home" (Matthew 13:57). Just because one person or organization doesn't want what you have to offer, that doesn't mean God won't use you somewhere else. You must be willing to be rejected, like Jesus was rejected, trusting that as you continue to tell the story, God will bring the right people to listen.

We are called to walk in humility. Passing on the church to our thirty-five-year-old son required us to exercise humility. We had to let go of some of our expectations and choose to believe that God had equipped our son to do the job in ways only he could. Alvin wasn't my baby boy anymore. He wasn't even the young man searching for his purpose and identity. Over the past ten years, God had been growing his faith and leadership skills. Alvin was ready to reach *his* generation for Christ in ways his father and I never could.

The Bible has a lot to say about humility. Proverbs 22:4 says, "Humility is the fear of the LORD; its wages are riches and honor and life." Fearing God results in humility—the realization that we know so little compared to an all-knowing, powerful God. Humility brings good things into our lives: riches and honor and life. God honors those who walk in humility. James 4:10 tells us, "Humble yourselves before the Lord, and he will lift you up." There is freedom and joy when we humble ourselves before God and allow Him to bring the successes.

As we handed over the lead pastor role to Alvin III, I knew there would be times when my husband and I would be tempted to impose our ideas on our son's leadership or try to convince him that we knew best. But those were moments to exercise humility and trust that God was working through him in ways we might not recognize or understand. We must open our eyes to see that the upcoming generations have good, God-inspired ideas. More than that, they are the people their generation needs. As we hold our own ways of doing things loosely, we can better empower the next generation to step fully into the unique calling God has for them.

In one of those first gatherings of young adults in our home, we were teaching on leadership and how they could lead the people around them. I remember the Holy Spirit whispering to my heart, "I want you to forget everything you think you know and be open to see what I'm going to do in this next generation." The generations after us won't do things the way we did them. We must always uphold scriptural truth and morals, but the way they run their race may look different than the way we ran ours. One thing I admire about the younger generation is their authenticity. They don't have to be perfect. I grew up feeling as though I had to be perfect before I could really be worthy and serve the Lord. That is a limiting belief. The Bible tells us we are being made perfect in Christ, but none of us has arrived. And as the younger generation embraces authentic faith—and doesn't wait for perfection before taking action—God will do amazing things through them. We must have the humility to allow them to be who God has called them to be, without trying to do the Holy Spirit's job.

PERFECT TIMING

When Alvin III became the lead pastor of Nashville Life Church at the start of 2021, it was a challenging time to be a pastor. He was required to navigate social and political tensions as well as the ongoing challenges of a global pandemic that had raised fears and brought grief and loss. As his father and I stepped back into the wings to offer support, we watched Alvin III step into his calling with confidence and poise.

When members of the congregation came to us, asking us questions about the church, we sent them to talk to Alvin. We let him run all the meetings and make all the decisions—sometimes not the same decisions we would have made. Releasing the reins wasn't always easy, but we understood it was essential. We prayed for our son daily. And then we watched.

I watched in awe as he rose to the challenge and the Lord used his clear, direct teaching and shepherd's heart to diffuse the disunity over hot-button topics. He expertly navigated the tension, exhorting us to turn our eyes to Jesus instead of our fears or the things dividing us.

Over time, I came to see that he was doing so many things better than we ever did. He was very effective at communicating with his own generation and able to stand firm under pressure.

Now I am filled with joy and gratitude at what the Lord has done. The church is thriving, and Alvin III is flourishing in his role. There have been challenges, of course, but God has made a way through each trial that has allowed us to see more of who He is and what He's calling us to. God is faithful through every generation, and He's given us the exciting task of equipping those who will carry on His message of hope when we are gone. May we do it with grace.

- What do we learn about mentorship from the example of Paul and Timothy?

  _____

  _____

  _____

- What role does honor play in passing down faith? What about humility?

  _____

  _____

  _____

- What are some ways Christians can strengthen intergenerational relationships?

  _____

  _____

  _____

CHAPTER

ten

BELIEVE FOR IT

In early 2020, when I agreed to do my first live record, I had no idea the world was about to shut down due to a global pandemic. Many of the songs on the album were already written and arranged before the stay-at-home orders took effect in March of that year. My management and producers determined that with or without a pandemic, this live worship performance needed to go on, and I'm incredibly grateful for their discernment.

By the end of summer, the songs were ready to go, but as I met with the producers, we still felt something was missing. The recording needed an anthem, a song that would be the theme of the record. We were of one mind on this, so I told them that if they could get a new song to me before the recording date, I would consider it.

One day, Kyle Lee, one of the producers, was mowing his lawn and thinking about what this song needed to be. What did the church need to hear in these extraordinary times? *We've just got to believe for this song*, he thought. That's when he felt the nudge from the Holy Spirit. *That's the song!* Believe for it. *People need to believe that God is still able to do the impossible.*

He pulled in Dwan Hill and Mitch Wong, and those three young, talented songwriters came up with a draft. The moment I heard the song, I was hooked. This was the anthem people needed. With everything going on in the world, I knew that many were evaluating if they truly believed. In such difficult times, Christians were asking, "When circumstances look hopeless, do I believe God is bigger?"

As I began fine-tuning the song and making my additions, I was reminded of Mark 11:22–24, where Jesus says: "Have faith in God. . . . Truly I tell you, if anyone says to this mountain, 'Go, throw yourself into the sea,' and does not doubt in their heart but believes that what they say will happen, it will be done for them. Therefore, I tell you, whatever you ask for in prayer, believe that you have received it, and it will be yours."

I wanted people to live by these words and take them at face value. When we believe for what God has promised,

He responds to our faith. All of this was taking place at the same time God was continuing to stir in my heart a sense of urgency for the next generation. They needed to decide for themselves that God was real. They couldn't just go on the faith of their parents; they needed to make their own confessions of faith. And if their answer was, "Yes, I believe it," then they needed to walk in it. The song "Believe For It" was timely. It was a call for all generations to take God at His Word and trust Him to do the impossible and carry them through whatever storms they might be facing.

God's timing is perfect. If my live recording had happened in May 2020 as originally planned, "Believe For It" would not have been on the record. I saw the Lord work through every challenge we encountered. As I look back on how even seemingly insignificant details fell into place, I'm reminded that when things don't go our way, God is still at work. He knows what needs to happen and when it needs to happen.

By the time the song was written, the world was in the thick of the pandemic. People were losing loved ones. Some were fighting for their lives. People couldn't even go to church, something we had taken for granted. People needed hope. They needed a "new song," as directed in Psalm 96:1, that would encourage them to hold on and not give up.

I chose twelve other worship songs I felt would draw people closer to God and deepen their faith in Him. Once we had settled on a playlist, my talented friends Calvin Nowell and Dwan Hill pulled together the musicians and background singers who would join me on stage. I trusted them to pick singers and musicians who had the heart of worship but were also skilled in the art of worship. They brought in phenomenal musicians they knew would feel a personal connection with this project. During one of our first rehearsals, held at my home, the singers talked about why this project was meaningful to them. I was blessed and surprised to hear how my music had made an impact on many of their lives. It was evident the Spirit had been working in all of us to take this message of hope into the world.

A few of the singers had been involved with my Always Sisters, Forever Brothers conference. Looking back, even then God was stirring in my heart a passion to see young people grow strong in their faith. From 2005 to 2011, I put on the conference at Belmont University to encourage the younger generation to live sold-out lives to Jesus. The conference featured inspiring guests, such as Tony Dungy, Dr. I.V. Hilliard, Lecrae, Maya Angelou, and many others. Over the years, thousands of teens and young adults attended the conference and devoted their lives to Christ.

When I first launched the conference, my friend and coworker Demetrus Alexander, along with other amazing young people, helped me make my vision into a reality—from singing on the worship team, to playing in the band, marketing the event, and selling merchandise. I've discovered there's something incredibly rewarding about working alongside young people for a kingdom assignment. Cheering each other on and seeing young people reaching their peers for Christ was so exciting and a great reminder of God's faithfulness to every generation.

AN UNUSUAL RECORDING

Making my first live record ended up being nothing like I'd imagined when I first agreed to it. Instead of a packed venue of 3,500 people, only fifty could attend that October 2020 evening. Once we knew we were putting on a live recording, I asked a small group of people to be intercessors for the project. That night, I invited them to the performance to pray during the recording while the others stood in front of the stage and worshipped with me. I knew this couldn't just be entertainment. People needed to have an encounter with Jesus.

I knew from the start that I wanted to create an experience. I wanted listeners and viewers to feel as if they were in a church service, since many of us had been kept from church during the pandemic. I told the Lord, "God, just let me capture Your Spirit. If I capture Your Spirit, then people are going to receive what they need." God answered that prayer. He took that intimate setting and did what only He could do. As we sang the tracks, I gave each one to God and asked Him to respond to our worship.

Spirit-directed singing is a Winans family tradition. The Winans is still my favorite gospel group, and when I was younger, I used to go to my brothers' concerts. We called my older brother, Marvin, the "Vamp-pire," because every song had a vamp. A vamp happens when you improvise. You sing the song and then just sit there a minute and think, *What else can this song do?* The Holy Spirit gives you a thought, and you follow the wind. The wind might go somewhere different than you planned, and you just go there with it. I gave myself that freedom during the live performance, and the Spirit showed up.

Knowing my tendencies, Calvin was careful to bring in singers who could be flexible when I improvised. I wanted the performance to be interactive between the Lord, the listener, and the musicians. Partway through the performance, I brought the singer-songwriter MDSN (pronounced "Madison") up on stage. She was nineteen at the time and had been writing music since she was nine. She even turned down talks with interested Disney Channel music executives because God had placed a specific calling on her life. In her words, "I want to see people's lives changed. To be an influencer for my generation and to make music that helps Christians deepen their faith while introducing others to Jesus."[1]

I had selected her song "Hunger" to be on my live album because every time we sang it at Nashville Life, I felt we were in the throne room of God. I have found that when a song ministers to my heart, I'm able to minister more deeply to other people. During the performance, I brought MDSN up to sing part of her beautiful song.

"I wasn't trying to do this song better, because I know I can't," I said facing her on the stage. "I'm doing it because I want people to experience the anointing that's in this song. I'm a worshipper. And I want you to know God has used you to take my worship to another level."

I handed her the mic, and she began to sing part of her song in a higher key than I could manage. As we stood there listening to her ethereal voice, I thought about how this young woman is our future. She has already made

---

1. "Integrity Music Welcomes Teen Artist MDSN," Gospel Music Association, August 2, 2017, https://gospelmusic.org /integrity-music-welcomes-teen-artist-mdsn/.

tough decisions to follow Christ. Even the fact that she sang the song in a different key than me felt symbolic. When I am gone, MDSN and young women and men like her will carry the torch, spreading the gospel in ways I never could.

That's why I'm so passionate about collaborating with young people. The producers and cowriters of "Believe For It" are the upcoming generation. I've had the privilege of collaborating with Lauren Daigle, Carrie Underwood, Tauren Wells, and celebrated youth choirs and singing groups. I love working with the next generation and putting together our unique gifts and talents to create something that inspires people to have a closer walk with Christ.

GOD OF ALL GENERATIONS

The longer I live, and the more people I meet, the more I recognize that every generation has its challenges. A global pandemic only highlighted some of the great difficulties and hurts, such as depression, anxiety and loneliness, our young people are walking through. The enemy is crafty and constantly coming up with new tactics. Here's an example of one specific challenge: Those of us born before the digital age didn't have to contend with bullying on social media. We may have faced in-person bullying or even discrimination, but we didn't have to worry about it coming from a handheld device 24-7. Online bullying is a serious problem that has led to a myriad of mental health struggles and even an increase in suicide rates in our young people. Whereas in some previous generations, young people may have died in wars or as a result of being in a gang, today the enemy has modified his tactics to exploit an ever-widening circle of issues plaguing our kids.

The enemy's mission is consistent: steal, kill, and destroy. But his methods are ever-changing, and he enacts his carnage in different ways for different generations. We must constantly be alert to his strategies. He uses the currency of confusion, division, chaos, anger, and hate. Where we find these things, we can be sure he is at work. Despite his gains, avoiding his schemes is actually very simple. James 4:7 tells us how: "Submit yourselves, then, to God. Resist the devil, and he will flee from you."

Submit yourselves to God. He's a God of *every* generation. His Word works every day. It worked back then, and it will work until Jesus returns. The power of God is still the power of God, and it is the greatest power by far. In this present age, He's still the everlasting Father. He still knows all things. He's still the King of kings and Lord of lords. He's not diminished. He's not watered down. He's not afraid. And nothing takes Him by surprise.

Our young people need to know this is the God in whom we place our trust. A great God who sits on a throne. Our world is dark, but God is not afraid of darkness; He pushes it back. As we submit to Him, we can experience complete victory over darkness. To the Christians in Rome, Paul wrote, "The God of peace will soon crush Satan under your feet" (Romans 16:20). Jesus won the battle a long time ago—He finished it. And it's still finished.

When I had Tamara Bennett (Tammy to me, and the daughter of our childhood pastor, Pastor Stacks) on the *Generations* show to talk about passing on faith, we discussed generational blessings and curses. She made a powerful point: "Sin cursed us all," she said. "His grace cuts the curse." Even things that appear good, such as religion, can be a curse, she reminded us, because religiosity is a form of godliness without power (2 Timothy 3:5). "The curse is broken when I accept Jesus Christ," she said. "That curse is over. That's what we take to the next generation." While generational curses are real, all curses are broken through Jesus Christ.

Romans 8:2 says, "Through Christ Jesus the law of the Spirit who gives life has set you free from the law of sin and death." The same grace that broke the curse when Jesus rose victorious from the grave breaks the curse today. So whether I accepted Jesus fifty years ago or today, the curse is lifted and I can walk in freedom.

We must stop believing what society says about our kids and believe the report of the Lord. Acts 2:17 tells us our sons and daughters will prophesy. Our children are the head and not the tail (Deuteronomy 28:13). And they can do all things through Him who gives them strength (Philippians 4:13).We must keep believing God is who He says He is and that He will be that for our children. His faithfulness is not contingent on our choices or a cultural moment. He is the same yesterday, today, and forever (Hebrews 13:8), and He'll continue to be faithful to every generation.

MODELS OF FAITH

At the Generations Live conference, I had all my speakers, along with my mother, Delores Winans, and my daughter, Ashley Phillips, come on stage to record a live *Generations* show for YouTube. Toward the end of our discussion, the moderator asked each woman on the stage to tell us how we could pray for her. Some of the women asked us to pray for wisdom for making big life decisions or pruning commitments from their lives. Others asked for prayer for the ability to be still and listen to the Lord in the upcoming days. I asked for prayer for discernment as I led Generations.

Among these petitions, my eighty-five-year-old mother's request stood out: "I ask for the Lord to give me patience and guidance and wisdom for what I need to do today. I pray that He would order my steps and show me what I need to do and who I need to tell. I don't want to rust out. I want to be used until I leave here." Instead of asking for something that would make her life easier or more fruitful, she simply asked for the stamina to run her race well to the finish. Then she offered a word to the women in attendance:

> I thank God for my life in Him. I found Him when I was young, and in serving the Lord, I missed a lot of pitfalls. The Lord offers life or death. When I said, "I believe the Lord Jesus Christ is my Savior," I meant it. My word to the younger women is this: Fall in love with the Lord. Fall in love with His Word. Believe the Word of

the Lord. He had the answer when I was seventeen, and He still has the answer today.

Every woman in that room hung on every word that came out of my mother's mouth. They were hungry for her testimony and time-tested wisdom. She has been places with the Lord that we have never been. She has seen Him do things we have never seen. Because of that, she carries spiritual authority. Her words are credible.

When I was growing up, I wanted to be like my mother. Even as a child, I understood that her beauty came from God dwelling in her. The law of kindness was on her tongue. I never had to guess what it meant to be a godly woman. Her love for Jesus was evident.

God provided other role models from the older generation as well. I looked forward to attending Bible study on Tuesday and Thursday night to hear Pastor Stacks preach the truths of God's Word. I'd bring my notebook and pen and take notes as fast as I could. Sometimes it felt as if smoke was coming off my pencil from writing so fast! At those meetings, God's Word truly was sweeter than honey to my mouth (Psalm 119:103). It left me wanting more. And by the time I returned on Thursday, I would have seen the Word of God in action in the events of my life. I didn't know it then, but those messages would affect me for the rest of my life.

And I must mention once again my Grandmother Howze. For many years, she was my best friend. I hung out with her and the other mothers of the church and would accompany her to 6:00 a.m. prayer before school. That's where I first experienced the presence of God and learned to crave it. Even as a child, I recognized that those dear older women had peace and joy and the presence of God.

Psalm 16:11 says, "You make known to me the path of life; you will fill me with joy in your presence, with eternal pleasures at your right hand." Because of those women, I never wondered if I was missing out. I knew God's presence was the most joyful place to be because I'd experienced it through the adults in my life.

Now it's my turn. I get to be that person in someone else's life. Passing on faith, while a sacred responsibility, is not complicated. As we take what has been handed down to us and walk in relationship with Christ, we naturally invite others to experience the Lord's goodness. We set the blueprint they can follow. As they watch us go through the ups and downs of life, biblical principles come alive.

The power is in coming together—learning from the generation ahead and pouring into the generation coming behind. We do this in many ways, including through mentorship, the strengthening of family bonds, service in the church, and community outreach. However, we must keep in mind that passing on faith is less about what we do and more about who we are. Second Corinthians 2:14 describes the knowledge of God as an aroma, something that tangibly permeates a space. This was what I felt when I joined my grandmother for morning prayer and soaked up the godliness of those church mothers. It's what I felt sitting in the church pews next to my siblings. And it's what I felt growing up in that small home that busted at the seams with love and joy.

When you've experienced the atmosphere of God's love, holiness, hope, peace, laughter, and wellness, you want to create that for others. When you take your eyes off yourself and look for somebody you can be a blessing to, blessings will increase in your life. When she was on the show, Tamara (Stacks) Bennett blessed me by sharing how my life had affected her. During some of her teenage struggles and doubts, she was watching. "I saw that you and your sisters were beautifully saved, and that became my hope," she said.

You never know who may be looking to you for hope today. Jesus declared we are the light of the world, a city on a hill that cannot be hidden (Matthew 5:14). We must not underestimate how brightly we shine in a dark world. We will never hear about some of the biggest ways God uses us, but we can be sure that as we proclaim His goodness, He will always do His part.

SONG OF HOPE

The live concert titled *Believe For It* made its debut on the Trinity Broadcasting Network on March 19, 2021, almost one year to the day from when nationwide lockdowns went into effect. The response was overwhelming; messages poured in describing how the music had arrived just in time. The "Never Lost" lyric video, produced by Cmon Creative, released as a single before the live concert and received one million views in the first three months.

When the *Believe For It* live performance won three Grammy Awards on April 3, 2022, I was stunned and overjoyed. I felt such deep gratitude to the amazing team of people who had made it possible. Who would have ever imagined I would record my first live collection during a global pandemic? But what is more meaningful to me than any award are the testimonies from people

We're in a time when we cannot back up. We must stand firm and believe for all that God will do in the next generation.

———————

around the world whose lives have been changed. I asked the Lord that the album capture His Spirit, and I believe it did. I give all the glory to God.

As I look back on my life, God has been faithful in every stage. I included "Goodness of God" in my live performance because it expresses so well how I feel about what God has done. From growing up in David and Delores Winans's family and enjoying a successful career in music, to meeting my husband, raising a family, and founding a church—God has been so good.

His closeness as my Father and my Friend has given me hope and inspired me to praise Him with my song and my life. I have learned that God is always faithful. His love conquers hate. His tenderness mends broken hearts. His compassion never fails. We must be convinced that God is able to do what He said He will do. I want to pass all of that on to my children so that they will be the house that's built on the rock and stand firm through the storms of life.

I love seeing the raw faith of my children's generation. Their faith looks different than mine, but they have what it takes for the cultural moment in which God has placed them. I believe God equips every generation for what that generation needs. He shapes us for our harvest. We just need to be faithful to plant the seeds and nurture them. God will make them grow. We learn from the past and honor those who've gone before us, but there's always so much more to discover. As we take what the Lord has given us and pour it into others, we will see His mighty acts and praise them to our children.

We're in a time when we cannot back up. We must stand firm and believe for all that God will do in the next generation. I'm believing for miracles to happen. And I'm not waiting until I see them; I'm going to praise God for them now.

QUESTIONS *to* CONSIDER

- Who are some of your models of faith?

  _____

  _____

  _____

  _____

- What are some ways you can invest in the next generation?

  _____

  _____

  _____

  _____

- What are you believing for God to do today?

  _____

  _____

  _____

  _____

ACKNOWLEDGEMENTS

I want to first give thanks to my Heavenly Father for His steadfast love and faithfulness to every generation. God, I love You with all my heart, soul, and mind because You were kind enough to first love me. Thank you, Jesus, for paying the ultimate price so I could experience abundant life through no goodness of my own. By your grace, I am who You say I am.

I would like to thank my husband, Alvin Love II, for your support and encouragement. You have been a faithful partner and friend, a wonderful father and grandfather. We have adventured together through the highs and lows of many seasons, and I am so grateful to be walking by your side.

Thank you to my children—Alvin III and Ashley, and son-in-law, Kenny. I am so proud of you and blessed to see you walking diligently with Christ and proclaiming His goodness to your generation and the next. Thank you, Wyatt, for your unconditional love, worship dance parties, and sweet morning wake-up calls.

I thank my parents, David and Delores Winans, for their faithful, godly example. Dad, you were the foundation of our home. You made everything fun, and taught me to always praise the Lord. I still love and miss you. Mom, your steady love and perseverance in the faith has made me who I am today. I love you with all my heart. Thanks to my Grandma Howze for being my best friend. Thanks to my siblings—David, Ronald, Carvin, Marvin, Michael, Daniel, BeBe, Angie and Debbie—who helped shape me and show me what it means to be an imperfect family loving the Lord and growing in grace. I understand how very blessed I was to grow up with you all—in a place full of love, faith, music, and laughter. You have never stopped encouraging me, and I thank God for you.

Suzanne Gosselin, thank you for sharing your God-given talent and allowing Him to use you to bring this vision to life. I believe many will be blessed because of you.

Thank you to the team at EMF Publishing / K-LOVE Books. Dave Schroeder, thank you for your enthusiasm for this project and heart for people to experience the transforming power of Jesus. Jenaye Merida, I am grateful for your excellence and energy in managing the details and marketing of this book.

ACKNOWLEDGEMENTS

Thank you to the Dexterity team, Matt West, Kim West, Karen Longino, and Sarah Siegand. You have been extremely gracious, and it is a joy to work with you.

Thank you to my management, the MWS Group— Greg Ham, Madeline Halm and Derek Spirk—I am so grateful for how you have led the way and helped this book become a reality.

Thank you Zahraa for assisting every step of the way and for offering tech support.

Finally, I would like to thank all the mothers, elders, deacons, saints, and friends who invested in me and took the time to build me up and love me enough to pray for me, correct me, and train me in the faith. I am who I am because of you.

Love, CeCe

Stay up to date with music, events, and tours at
cecewinans.com

Voices that sing, teach and now... **podcast.**

FAITH-BASED PODCASTS

SCAN HERE TO LISTEN

HERE ARE MORE GREAT WAYS TO BE ENCOURAGED EVERYWHERE YOU GO!

POSITIVE, ENCOURAGING

K-LOVE

Download the app
or listen online at **KLOVE.com**

worship now

Download the app
or listen online at **Air1.com**

accessmore.
FAITH-BASED PODCASTS

Download the app
or listen online at **AccessMore.com**

Learn more about our books at
KLOVE.COM/BOOKS and **AIR1.COM/BOOKS**